WEIRD CRESCENTA VALLEY

HISTORICAL AND NATURAL ODDITIES

Mike Lawler

AMERICA THROUGH TIME®
ADDING COLOR TO AMERICAN HISTORY

America Through Time is an imprint of Fonthill Media LLC
www.through-time.com
office@through-time.com

Published by Arcadia Publishing by arrangement with Fonthill Media LLC
For all general information, please contact Arcadia Publishing:
Telephone: 843-853-2070
Fax: 843-853-0044
E-mail: sales@arcadiapublishing.com
For customer service and orders:
Toll-Free 1-888-313-2665

www.arcadiapublishing.com

First published 2022

ISBN 978-1-63499-431-6

Typeset in Sabon LT Std
Printed and bound in England

Contents

1
Weird Supernatural

Some Haunted Places in C.V.

Whether you are a believer or not, nearly everyone has either experienced the paranormal themselves or knows somebody who has, or at least thought they had. The paranormal is a pervasive part of our culture. It is in our legends and our literature. The Crescenta Valley is particularly ripe for hauntings. The Native Americans that lived here who did not die of painful European diseases were ripped violently from their culture. Many of our first American residents were tuberculosis sufferers, who, after being shunned by family and friends, died lonely and gasping for breath in local sanitariums. Scores of people died violently when the flood of 1934 ripped through the dark night.

Two stories come from the top of Briggs Avenue, where many tuberculosis victims died. A resident there told me they had been awakened several times by a man standing over their bed, sometimes lifting the bed slightly, who would soon fade away. Their house is exactly where Utley Sanitarium was, a tuberculosis hospital. The author's teenaged daughter and a friend were driving down Briggs Avenue one night, when two figures in white robes darted across the street directly in front of her car. She braked hard, and the two figures, illuminated in her headlights, ran straight into, and through, the side of a parked motorhome. The two girls screamed all the way down the hill.

A legendary ghost supposedly haunts C.V. High School's auditorium. The story goes that a few decades ago, on (of course) a dark and stormy night, while a play was being performed, a homeless guy snuck in the side door to get out of the rain. He hid in the equipment room below the stage and he died there. His ghost has been encountered by generations of kids.

Several years ago, I did an interview with a resident of Mountain Oaks. She told me that a regular visitor in her home was the ghost of one of the many Native Americans who were exploited by the Spanish for their labor. This one had been put to work cutting granite in the Verdugo Mountains, been hanged from a nearby oak tree for some minor offence, and buried near her house.

On the retail side of ghosts, we have the current Montrose Starbucks. It was originally a bank, with a below-ground vault. Generations of retail workers there, when it was later a dress shop and other retail ventures, report various "encounters" in the former vault.

As I said before, Crescenta Valley has had its share of untimely deaths, so there are lots of opportunities for disturbed spirits to take up residence.

Is Ralphs Supermarket Haunted?

This author has been hearing ghost stories from former employees of Ralphs Supermarket in La Crescenta. The stories are always from former employees, as there seems to be a hesitancy to talk by current employees, worried perhaps by blow-back from corporate. With that in mind, I will keep the stories anonymous.

Ralphs is built directly over the former site of Kimball Sanitarium, an insane asylum that ran from the mid-1920s until about 1960. It was torn down and the shopping center rose in its place. The asylum's origins ranged back to around 1922, when the Kimball family purchased a looming old Victorian house on a large parcel at Foothill and Raymond. They purpose-built several cottages for calmer patients, but for the violent ones, they built a cement block-house, featuring padded cells and wall-mounted restraints. Bela Lugosi is said to have received treatment for morphine addiction here, and tragic film star Francis Farmer spent nine months here, receiving brutal insulin shock therapy. The main house would have been towards the rear of today's Ralphs, while the block-house would have been about where the store's bakery is today. I suppose this sets the stage nicely for some hauntings.

Indeed, there are many spooky stories. Former employees, mostly those who worked the night shift stocking shelves, claim that they hear someone whispering in their ears as they work. Visual sightings of ghosts have been almost entirely of a lone woman. She is sometimes described as a blonde woman, and other times as a woman wearing a long white wedding dress. In two cases, a worker followed the woman. Reportedly, she walked down an aisle to the back of the store, then ascended a staircase in the backroom. In both reports, the woman disappeared when she reached the top. The woman has been seen in the back rooms by others. There is even one long-time female employee who reported that for ten years she had regular conversations with the ghostly woman. It was not reported what they talked about.

Could this be the ghost of blond actress Francis Farmer? After her movie and stage career spiraled into personal chaos in 1943, she was held at Kimball Sanitarium for nine months of repeated insulin shock therapy before she left. From there, she was committed to a mental hospital in Washington state, where according to her autobiography she was raped and brutalized. Farmer was married three times and tragically divorced from her cheating first husband just before her stay in Kimball, which could explain the wedding dress.

The only sighting of a man was when a night worker was sweeping the floor in the floral section. They were backing up as they worked and bumped into someone. When they turned, they were confronted by a man with no face. Obviously, they fled and reportedly would never work that area again.

This was Kimball Sanitarium in 1925. This is where the modern Ralphs Supermarket sits today at Foothill and Raymond. (*Glendale History Room, Library, Arts & Culture Dept., Glendale, CA*)

Other paranormal activity in the store has been freezer doors that open and close on their own, and storage room doors that swing open when there is no wind. One night worker reports that during a power outage, he braved a visit to the restroom in the backroom. While in there, he heard a locker door slam loudly. No one else was back there, and this particular locker is never used. My personal favorite story is that workers stocking shelves at night would hear loud scratching and knocking coming from the next aisle, where no one was working. Was this the spirit of someone locked in a padded cell scratching to get out?

These are just stories of course, and I suppose bored night workers can get creative. Yet consider this: if Ralphs is haunted by the patients of the sanitarium that was on the site, perhaps other supermarkets have similar tales. Do workers at Vons in Montrose, built over old Indian Springs swimming pool, find wet footprints on the aisle floors? Are the aisles of Vons La Crescenta store, built over the site of Verdugo Hills Bowl, plagued with the sound of rolling bowling balls and falling pins?

Rockhaven Sanitarium Ghost Stories

As most of us in C.V. already know, Rockhaven Sanitarium is one of the brightest stars in the valley's history. From 1923 to 2006, Rockhaven provided the absolute best of care to women with mild mental disabilities. Ladies who had often lived lives of great achievement were able to finish out their worldly time there with happiness and dignity. It is often said that Rockhaven was such a nice place that some residents would not leave, even after they died. When the volunteer docents, the "Friends of Rockhaven," give their tours of the now abandoned sanitarium, a portion of the tour covers the many ghostly encounters collected over the years since the city of Glendale bought the property in 2008.

When Glendale first bought the property, they were given a "real estate disclosure form" that stated that the previous owners' security guard was convinced that the place was haunted. The guard reported that at night he could hear the sound of furniture moving around the locked buildings and other odd sounds. The city of Glendale, on taking possession of the property, hired a no-nonsense retired cop as a security guard. He stated quite matter-of-fact that he was regularly seeing people out of the corner of his eye, but when he turned to look at them, they disappeared.

The author has been inside Rockhaven many times to assist with the cleaning and maintenance of the now mothballed facility. I am not a true believer myself (call me "agnostic" on spirits), and for the most part, the place still feels like the loving, caring place it always was. Yet there is one building that seems creepy, the so-called "Little Hospital," where many residents spent their last days. One day I was in that building by myself, cleaning the bathroom. As I swept years of dust from a series of shelves there, I found a little pile of crumbling pills in a back corner of the top shelf—evidence that someone decades ago was resisting treatment, perhaps "cheeking" their medication and then hiding it in the back corner of the top shelf. Just as I swept the remains of the pills into a dustpan, I distinctly "felt" someone walk up behind me, with a great deal of anger. Of course, when I turned around, there was no one there, and the sense of disembodied anger faded. Apparently, I had "caught" the lady who had been resisting her medication.

Over the years, I have heard a litany of odd tales from the various security guards and caretakers that have spent nights there. Live-in caretakers have reported that lights

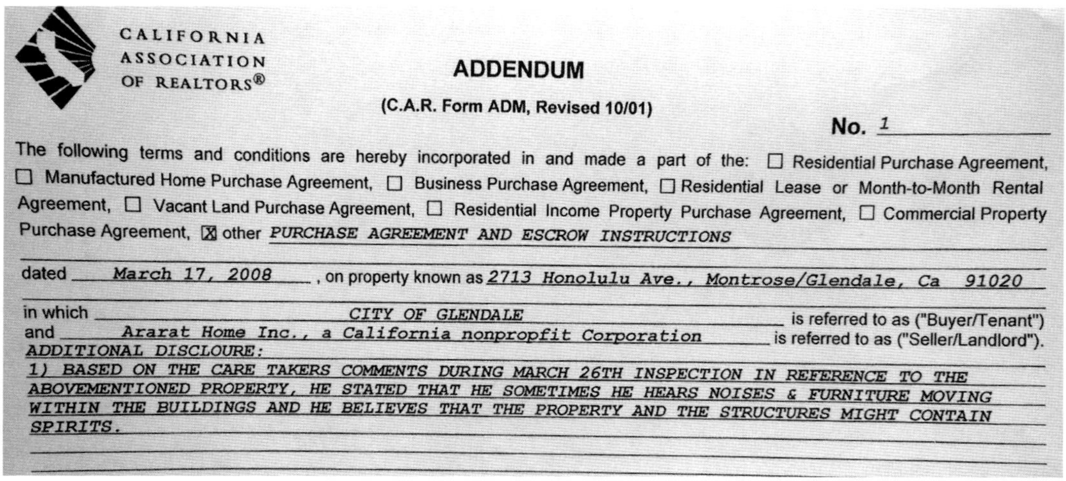

CALIFORNIA ASSOCIATION OF REALTORS®

ADDENDUM

(C.A.R. Form ADM, Revised 10/01)

No. 1

The following terms and conditions are hereby incorporated in and made a part of the: ☐ Residential Purchase Agreement, ☐ Manufactured Home Purchase Agreement, ☐ Business Purchase Agreement, ☐ Residential Lease or Month-to-Month Rental Agreement, ☐ Vacant Land Purchase Agreement, ☐ Residential Income Property Purchase Agreement, ☐ Commercial Property Purchase Agreement, ☒ other PURCHASE AGREEMENT AND ESCROW INSTRUCTIONS

dated March 17, 2008, on property known as 2713 Honolulu Ave., Montrose/Glendale, Ca 91020

in which CITY OF GLENDALE is referred to as ("Buyer/Tenant")
and Ararat Home Inc., a California nonpropfit Corporation is referred to as ("Seller/Landlord").

ADDITIONAL DISCLOURE:
1) BASED ON THE CARE TAKERS COMMENTS DURING MARCH 26TH INSPECTION IN REFERENCE TO THE ABOVEMENTIONED PROPERTY, HE STATED THAT HE SOMETIMES HE HEARS NOISES & FURNITURE MOVING WITHIN THE BUILDINGS AND HE BELIEVES THAT THE PROPERTY AND THE STRUCTURES MIGHT CONTAIN SPIRITS.

When a property is sold, it is the seller's responsibility to disclose anything "unusual" about the property. When Rockhaven was sold to the city of Glendale in 2008, the seller used this form to disclose that their security guard thought Rockhaven was haunted. (*Friends of Rockhaven*) would turn on or off, doors open and close, and locked windows would unlatch and swing open. Clocks would change time. Knocking on the walls occurred frequently.

One caretaker who lived on the Rockhaven property had many interactive ghost sightings. He and his wife, when in opposite sides of the house, would sometimes hear the other calling their name from nearby, and *vice versa*, as though the spirits were mischievously playing jokes on the couple. When the couple's relatives visited, they encountered the ghosts. When a cousin was visiting, he asked the caretaker who the lady was that was laying on the bed in their bedroom. He said she looked right at him when he passed by the door. The caretaker's mother looked out the kitchen window only to see a woman in a long old-fashioned dress look straight at her and beckon to her, inviting her to come outside.

We have had several ghost-hunter groups tour the grounds. They are not allowed (by the city of Glendale) to do full investigations with all their equipment, only take a tour, but many of the ghost hunters report sensing "great confusion" on the part of the spirits there. That fits, as many Rockhaven patients had Alzheimer's or dementia.

Bob McFall, the former Glendale assistant city manager, tells a couple of his own ghost stories from when Rockhaven was first purchased by the city in 2008. Bob was an amateur photographer and spent many of his off hours photographing the abandoned sanitarium. One day, he had his tripod set up next to a locked two-story building, the second floor of which had become the repository for all the resident's personal items that had been left behind. Unlike other times he had spent at Rockhaven, he felt like he was being watched. As he took his photos, he instinctively kept glancing up at a particular second-story window, and each time he looked up, he felt like the curtains were in a slightly different position. Finally, he looked up, caught the curtains slightly parted, and saw a woman peering down at him from the darkened room. He swung his camera up and snapped a photo, then went to investigate who was inside the locked building. Of course, no one was there. In the photo, there is an indistinct shadowy something caught in the window, but it is very faint. Some say it looks like a person, others not.

The "Friends of Rockhaven" volunteers clean the interiors on a regular basis, and so are very familiar with the appearance of each room. Lately, we have had a few items mysteriously appear. A valentine, a program from a granddaughter's dance recital, a "Rockhaven Dollar" (a coupon for treats), and a set of Rosary beads have lately all shown up in very obvious places, not during cleaning sessions, but while tours are going on. All of these have appeared just before a tour, as though the past residents were reaching out, saying, "Look at this, everyone! This was important to me."

Another story involves a piano that had been located in the dining hall, which shows up in many decades-old Rockhaven photos as a center of activity. Hundreds of women over the years must have discovered forgotten musical talents or sang old songs around that old upright. Yet when the city took over the property, they did a very careful inventory, but no piano showed up. The previous owners must have sold it or taken it with them. In the next few months, the piano was forgotten, as the city moved the huge inventory of valuable outdoor vases and garden art into a locked garage for safe-keeping. Bob McFall was kept busy conducting V.I.P. tours of Rockhaven for city staff and always made a point of finishing his tours by unlocking the garage to show off

The hallways of Rockhaven Sanitarium are dark and empty. Scenes like this do tend to get the imagination going. (*Author*)

the amazing collection of statuary and garden art. One day, he unlocked the garage for a tour, only two days after he had been in there with another tour. He swung the door up, and there in the middle of the floor sat the piano—the 700-lb piano that had previously been seen only in photos had mysteriously appeared in a locked room.

There is a whole section of paranormal research that deals with physical objects that appear from the past. That is possibly what is going on at Rockhaven Sanitarium. It is as though the past residents are reaching out to a new generation, to attempt to communicate how special Rockhaven was to them.

The Miracle of La Crescenta—Fireproof Ananda Ashrama

November 21, 1933—It was a quiet Tuesday evening at the Ananda Ashrama after a long hot summer. In the cool solitude of the 120-acre spiritual retreat at the top of Pennsylvania Avenue, the ashrama sisters read, sewed, or meditated. Around 1 mile away in Pickens Canyon, a fire of mysterious origin flared. Fanned by increasing Santa

Ana winds and fueled by brush that had not burned in decades, the inferno swept across Briggs Terrace, burning a few homes. It then charged northwest across the face of the San Gabriel Mountains towards the ashrama.

Firefighters streamed in from all parts of L.A. through the night, and the hundreds of young men housed in the three Civilian Conservation Corps units in the area were mobilized. The fire burned through the Bissell Estate at the top of La Crescenta Avenue that night and began to lick at the edges of the ashrama property. Hundreds of firefighters made a valiant stand and stopped the flames. At dawn, the wind began to die and the fire retreated up the mountain. The jubilant sisters fed the exhausted firemen, thinking the danger had passed. The experienced firefighters knew better, knowing that when the Santa Ana winds returned at sunset, the smoldering hillside would reignite. That day, they arrayed their hoses and pumpers around the compound.

As the firemen had predicted, sunset brought a great gust of wind, which fanned the glowing embers alive. Almost immediately, a 50-foot-high wall of flame shot into the air from the canyons next to the ashrama. The firefighters were overwhelmed by the sudden ferocity of the gusting firestorm. The wind had an insane intensity to it, sending flames over and around the ashrama. The fire got away from the firefighters, and they, and the sisters, found themselves surrounded—cut off from escape. The fire chief directed the sisters to shelter in the cloister. The chief entered the cloister doorway, the flames visible behind him, and told the women, "The fire is going to strike us, but we will do our best to save you." The chief stepped back outside, and as the landscaping at the edges of the cloister began to burn, he instructed his men to save the women. He directed them to array themselves in a circle around the cloister, to lay flat on their stomachs while covering their faces, and spray their hoses on the structure. The bushes at their outstretched feet began to explode like match heads.

Inside the cloister, the women knelt and began to pray. The darkened room lit up like daylight as showers of flaming embers poured down on the structure. The fire roared outside as smoke began to seep through the closed windows and the temperature rose. The women chanted in unison, and the fire-engulfed house seemed to vibrate with the intensity of their prayers. But the fire quickly passed over and the roaring subsided. The chief reentered the room and in a shaking voice announced, "The fire has gone over. It was the hand of God that saved you."

Morning broke to an amazing scene. The several structures of the ashrama were untouched by fire while everything around was burned—little islands in a sea of white ash. The bushes at the base of the temple walls were consumed, but of the building, only the edges of the eaves showed scorch marks. The flames had touched the foundations of the many cabins with their shake roofs, but nothing on them had ignited. The community house was surrounded by highly combustible eucalyptus trees, but the trees and the house were untouched. The brush burned right next to the cow barn filled with dry hay, which should have exploded but did not. The wooden steps to a house that was part of the compound burned halfway up and then miraculously stopped.

Headlines the next day proclaimed that the ashrama and the firefighters were trapped and probably dead because no one could have survived that inferno, but in reality, all were unhurt. One smoky firefighter proclaimed: "I am not a religious man, but I am convinced those prayers saved us all." It was perhaps a miracle.

A Ghostly Wife Leads a Grieving Husband to Her Lost Corpse

As we delve into the records of the Ananda Ashrama, a religious retreat at the top of Pennsylvania Avenue, we find yet another tale of the supernatural. This one involves Phillip and Ruth Reihl, a La Crescenta couple in their thirties who were followers of the ashrama's Swami Paramananda.

At exactly midnight on New Year's Eve 1933, a cloudburst of Biblical proportions was unleashed on the fire-denuded San Gabriels. In the inky blackness of midnight, the mountainside cut loose and sent roaring walls of mud and rocks (debris flows) speeding down and across the valley, killing scores of people and destroying hundreds of homes. The ashrama dodged that disaster, sustaining only minor damage to its water system, while on either side of the property, homes were swept away. Not so lucky were Phillip and Ruth Reihl, whose home in the 2600 block of Piedmont Avenue sat directly in the path of the Pickens Canyon debris flow, the deadliest of the seven debris flows that cut swaths across the Crescenta Valley.

Just after midnight, as the heavy rain poured down, Phillip and Ruth embraced and cooed "Happy New Year!" in the warm, dry comfort of their little home. As they held each other, the ground began to shake, and a roaring sound like a speeding train approached quickly from the northeast. The noise and shaking reached a crescendo as a wall of massive boulders and mud slammed into their house, bursting through the front wall. Ruth was wrenched violently from Phillip's grasp, and he heard her shriek "Oh my God!" Phillip was then thrust to the back of the house, where his legs and arms were shredded as he was shoved through a hole in the stucco wire. He found himself being carried on the flow, bouncing on the top of rolling, moving boulders, grasping ineffectually at tree limbs as he flew by them. Fortunately, he stayed on top and was not pulled into the churning "rock grinder" effect inside the debris flow that tore some bodies to pieces.

Two blocks downstream at Honolulu, he was thrown out of the main flow and up onto the steps of an intact house. Through the darkness, the occupant of the house saw the mud-covered form on his front steps. Not knowing if it was an animal or a human, he darted out and dragged the body inside. As he washed the mud from Phillip's face, he recognized an old friend, Sergeant Riehl, who had served with him in WWI—Phillip had landed in his old army commander's home.

Phillip was carried to an aid station, where after resting he set out into the dark night to search for Ruth. In physical and emotional agony, Phillip combed through wreckage from 3 a.m. until 11 a.m. looking for her. He stopped in the fire station to see if there was word of her. It was there in the relative calm of the station that Ruth's ghost appeared before Phillip. Wordlessly, her ghostly image raised an arm and pointed toward their home on Piedmont, then just as silently disappeared. Phillip stumbled across the torn landscape to the site of their home, where he found her hidden body tangled in the wreckage. After retrieving her corpse, he collapsed and was carried to the ashrama where he recuperated.

Ruth's body was cremated and spread in the Pacific. Phillip, after losing his wife of thirteen years, never remarried. His home gone, he lived on for several decades at the ashrama, becoming an indispensable member of their community, save for two years spent in India studying yoga. Phillip Riehl was forever grateful that his wife had returned briefly to ease his agony, and to give closure to her death.

Tujunga Ghost Stories

This author recently picked up a book called *Folk Tales of Sunland Tujunga*, a collection of local supernatural stories produced by the Little Landers Historical Society and available at their museum, Bolton Hall.

Two of the stories involve roads. The first is about an apparition that has been seen by several motorists in Big Tujunga Canyon. Always at night, the apparition is seen by the side of the highway about 2 miles above the second bridge, where the road steepens as it climbs up the canyon to Angeles Forest Highway. A man walking toward Tujunga is caught in the headlights of passing cars. If he is seen head-on, he smiles, sticks out his thumb, and waves frantically with the other hand. If approached from behind, he turns around as he is walking, and again puts out his thumb and waves, even jumping up and down to get the attention of the driver. Many people have stopped, thinking he is in need of help, but in each case, he seems to disappear as soon as they pull over. Despite waiting or even doubling back, the drivers find nothing but dark empty highway. Some drivers even reported that they felt like they were "being watched". Perhaps there was some tragedy on that treacherous highway. Maybe a car went over the side, and a victim of the accident is still trying to summon help.

A landmark on Sunland Boulevard since the 1930s is an old-world European-style restaurant. Old Vienna was its name for most of that time. Today it is Villa Terraza. Up until Sunland Boulevard was straightened and widened in the 1950s, there was a sharp S-curve in front of the restaurant that was the scene of several fatal accidents. Many drivers died on that spot. Today, a few drivers have reported that as they passed the restaurant at night, they have had to brake hard or swerve when an old-fashioned forties-styled car appeared in their headlights, and suddenly veered in front of them, or a seemingly drunk man staggered into the road in front of them. In all cases, nothing is found, save for the skid-marks of the modern car. Apparently, some forgotten accident is played out again and again on the dark road.

Another story involves a phantom airplane over Sunland Park. One afternoon in late December 1950, a Glendale family took their small plane for a sightseeing flight. They flew low and slow over Tujunga, then circled slowly over Sunland Park for about ten minutes. The pilot pulled the nose of the plane up to gain altitude, but it was too sharp a climb for their slow speed. The plane stalled, nosed over, and fell out of the sky. It smacked into the ground at the edge of Sunland Boulevard, right where the freeway crosses today. The wreckage burst into flame, and the five people aboard that were not killed on impact burned to death. In modern times, several witnesses have reported that they have heard a single-engine plane circling very low over Sunland Park. It is always near the end of December in the late afternoon. They can clearly hear the low-flying plane, but looking up toward the sound in the clear sky, they see nothing.

The last story took place in the McGroarty House. It is the former home of poet and writer John Steven McGroarty, but today is a museum and cultural center. Many photos exist of a favorite pet of McGroarty's, a big yellow cat. Volunteers were working in the house in the 1970s. A beam of light from the setting sun shone through a window, brightly illuminating a yellow cat. All saw the cat clearly as he looked around and then promptly disappeared. Perhaps he realized he was on the wrong plain of existence.

Apparitions take many forms in Tujunga—cars, planes, animals, and people. Keep a sharp eye out, and an open mind, when you are in Tujunga.

Alien Abductions in Tujunga

One of the earliest modern stories of extraterrestrial abductions came out of our own Big Tujunga Canyon. These abductions, which began in 1953, predate the more famous Betty and Barney Hill abductions of 1961, but they were not publicized until 1980 with the publication of *The Tujunga Canyon Contacts* by Ann Druffel and D. Scott Rogo.

The book details the stories of several women abductees, starting with the story of two young women sharing an isolated cabin in Big Tujunga Canyon on March 22, 1953. In the middle of the night, the two women were awaked by a very bright light that seemed to surround the cabin. They were both aware that time seemed to stand still, until they were finally able to break their seeming trance and flee. As they ran, one of the women spotted the filmy apparition of a long-haired man. Later on, hypnotists delved into the memories of these women, and those regressions unlocked stories of what happened during the period that "time seemed to stand still." Tales emerged of being taken onto alien craft and undergoing medical examinations by large-headed grey-skinned humanoid creatures. The women also reported further visits from the alien entities in subsequent years.

Four other cases involving alien contact with women in the Tujunga area are studied in the book, ranging from the original 1953 event up into the 1970s, with more fantastic tales of entities moving through solid walls and the abductees being floated into waiting spaceships. One of the women even reported being given a cancer cure by the aliens. In most of these cases, the abductees were visited repeatedly.

The later portion of the book details the various defense techniques to resist being abducted that these women developed over their many years of contacts with the extraterrestrials. Most involved mental strength through prayer, mantras, or other such mind-mastering tricks to ward off unwanted contact with these aliens.

In fact, the author, Ann Druffel, expanded this portion of her study of these cases into a subsequent book entitled *How to Defend Yourself Against Alien Abductions*. So, if the first book gets you worried about living so close to a hotbed of alien abduction, her second book will calm your fears.

UFO Sightings in Our Area

The earliest of these UFO sightings took place in May 1949. Two Glendale women watched a silver disc cross the afternoon sky over downtown Glendale at a high speed. It seemed to tilt and then suddenly disappeared. Later that month, again in broad daylight in the same area over downtown Glendale, eighteen different people all reported a disturbing sight. They all saw a semi-transparent oval-shaped object hovering over the city. It sat motionless in the sky for several minutes, emitting a faint noise like a motor. Then, just like the silver disc observed earlier, it seemed to tilt and then disappeared.

A year later in March 1950, many La Crescenta residents reported watching a large object slowly transit the morning sky. It was described as a "gondola-shaped object" attached to a light-colored triangular "hull." That same day in the late afternoon, several Burbank residents watched a "revolving wheel" in the sky above Burbank Airport, a wheel with shiny "spokes." The wheel flew quickly southwest and disappeared.

In 1952, several people in Eagle Rock watched a bizarre object slowly cross the sky to the north over the San Gabriel Mountains. It was described as a brilliant gold ball, streaming a red tail behind it. It was visible for several minutes.

On an overcast day in January 1954, a Glendale woman reportedly watched straight above her two brilliant blueish-white objects spinning around each other. The objects appeared to have sawtooth edges and were hovering just below the cloud cover for about fifteen minutes.

In 1955, thousands of people in the Crescenta Valley watched three round silver objects hovering high in the sky. Their positions seemed to constantly shift in relation to each other. They were visible for several hours. High-altitude weather balloons were suspected, but an investigation showed that none were in the area.

In 1955, three sheriffs from the Montrose Sheriff Station watched several flying saucers maneuvering over La Cañada and Flintridge in the late afternoon. According to the deputies, for forty-five minutes, they watched as the strange craft hovered, bunched, formed into figures, and flew over each other. Other calls were received by the Sheriff Station reporting the strange sight. In keeping with the Cold War mindset of that era, a call was made to Norton Air Force Base and fighter jets were scrambled. Just before the jets arrived over C.V., the objects merged into one and disappeared from view. The three deputies would not refute their sighting.

Two sighting were reported in the summer of 1957. Two Glendale men watched through binoculars as a strange object with a body and tail hovered over the Crescenta Valley for five minutes, then suddenly accelerated and disappeared over the San

Gabriels. A month later, someone in Glendale watched two jets over the C.V. area being followed by an orb with a dark center.

Ten years pass before another well-publicized sighting is reported, and it was a good one. One night in 1967, three friends in their twenties watched from the San Fernando Valley as a large disc-shaped object flew near them, several hundred feet off the ground. They followed it in their car, chasing it up through the Sunland/Tujunga area and into Big Tujunga Canyon. But while heading up the canyon road, their car broke down. Two of the group decided to follow on foot, while the third had seen enough and chose to walk back.

The pair—a young man and woman—followed the object up into an isolated part of the dark canyon. There, the disc halted and hovered near the ground. The pair cautiously approached to within a few hundred feet. Suddenly, a ball of fire rose up from a nearby hill, and what the two described as an electrical beam shot out from the ball up into the hills. After that shocking event, the saucer continued its way up the canyon. The pair tried to follow, but eventually lost it. The next morning, they walked back out of the canyon and reported their experience.

In the 1970s, there were several sightings of "phantom helicopters." They often appeared at the same time as UFOs. They resembled helicopters but did not appear to have rotors and did not make typical helicopter noises. They were always black and did not have lights.

On a summer evening in 1975 at about 8 p.m., residents of a home overlooking Big Tujunga Canyon heard a helicopter circling over the canyon. The wife and a visiting friend went out on their balcony to check it out. They could see the lights of the circling helicopter and were alarmed to see, about 1,000 feet above the helicopter, a round, brilliantly lit object. The helicopter was obviously watching the object as it circled.

They called the husband out to see this spectacle, and the three watched amazed as the bright object began to change its shape from round to diamond, then to a chevron, then to a classic saucer, as it somersaulted in the air. It then began to zig-zag above the helicopter, changing altitude abruptly up and down.

With this, the lone helicopter left, but soon, two more helicopters flying in formation came in and seemingly tried to follow the object's movements, but from a distance. In the dark, they saw occasional flashes in the cockpit of one of the copters as though someone was taking photos. Soon, two jets flew over at a higher altitude. Obviously, the object was attracting attention. At 10:30, bright lights went on higher up in the San Gabriels in the direction of a Nike missile base that had recently been deactivated. At this point, the object began to slowly move away, followed by the two helicopters, until they were out of sight of the people on their balcony.

Another night in February 1977, a police helicopter was patrolling above La Crescenta. The two officers aboard saw a bright yellow light pass below them at high speed, heading north. Thinking it was an airplane without proper lights, they followed it to investigate.

As soon as they turned to follow, the light zipped up to the same level as the helicopter and began to slowly circle the police copter about 300 feet away. Now the two police officers got a good look at the object. The yellow light was at the bottom of the craft, which was a dark upright cylinder about 15 feet high and 5 feet wide. They could clearly see what appeared to be struts of some sort attached to the cylinder.

After about two minutes of circling the helicopter, the object rose about 500 feet, darted off to the south, and vanished. The officers were startled by the rapidity that the mysterious object had disappeared. It was near a full moon that night, and if the object had simply turned off its light, they would have still have been able to see the object traveling away in the moonlight. One of the police officers stated afterward, "It didn't disappear into the distance as if it put on speed. One minute it was plainly visible, the next instant the light and cylinder weren't there."

Our area, and in particular Big Tujunga Canyon, seems to be a hotspot for UFO activity, including as mentioned in this chapter, one of the earliest (1953) alien abduction stories. These are wonderful stories. If you think they are true or not true is entirely up to you.

Does Bigfoot Live in the Mountains Above Us?

Bigfoot, or Sasquatch, is a legendary hulking 7–10-foot-tall hairy creature, somewhere between a man and an ape. It has been reported for hundreds of years worldwide, with many of the sightings in the Pacific Northwest. Yet there are several reported encounters in the last fifty years in the San Gabriel Mountains. Here are a handful of them, collected from the files of the Bigfoot Field Researchers Organization and the Angeles Sasquatch Association.

A few of the encounters were simply unexplained noises. An example of that occurred in 2002 high up in Big Tujunga Canyon when two hikers noticed a horrible smell like rotten eggs or a portable toilet. They were startled by a loud banging noise coming from a grove of trees above them, like a log being banged against a tree, and in fact the tops of the big oaks were swaying back and forth. Next a very loud wild groan or scream pierced the air, not human, but not like a bear either. The hikers retreated and the noise stopped, but each time they stopped to look back, the banging and screaming would start anew.

More dramatic are the several actual sightings. In the early 1970s, a group of deer hunters were traversing the side of a canyon near Mt. Waterman. They saw something climbing the other side of the canyon about 700 yards away and watched it through their rifle scopes. They said it looked like a "monkey man," somewhere between a human and a bear, very tall and weighing several hundred pounds, all brown, walking upright. The group watched it until it disappeared in the trees, but they were adamant that it was neither human or a bear. In the next few days, there were similar sightings in the Pearblossom area.

Another encounter was in 1976 near Morris Dam off Highway 39 above Azusa. The reservoir behind the dam is off limits, but two avid fishermen would regularly hop the fence at night. After a good night of fishing, they were following the faint trail back to their car. In the dark, they heard heavy footfalls on the trail in front of them. "It" stayed just ahead of them as they cautiously continued. They finally came to a clearing, and a huge, human-like creature was about 20 feet away looking back at them. The pair reported: "It turned 90 degrees up river and took off running through dense brush, in the black of night, like a running back for the Rams, like no human can!"

One of my favorite stories comes from a little farther afield, above Santa Clarita, but still in our San Gabriel Mountains. In 1980, two young men went on a last wilderness camping trip before reporting for army boot camp. They hiked 3 miles off San Francisquito Canyon Road and set up camp surrounded by thick brush. That night they were alarmed to hear the sound of something big crunching through the underbrush, slowly circling their campsite. Spooked, the two shined flashlights, yelled, and finally fired three rounds from their gun, but to no effect. "It" kept circling. They could not take it anymore and bolted. They ran the 3 miles back to the road, where they spent the rest of the night hiding in a drainage ditch.

With dawn, their courage returned, and they hiked back to their camp, intending to brave another night. But that evening at sunset, they encountered "it" again, standing 30 feet away facing them. It was 8 feet tall, with long arms and covered with hair. They saw it clearly as it gazed impassively at them. Then it turned and, slightly bent forward, slowly lumbered into the brush, making the same crunching noise they had heard the night before. The two spent another sleepless night before packing up and leaving the next morning.

There have been no Bigfoot encounters in the last decade. Perhaps our many recent wildfires drove our resident Sasquatch out for good, or maybe he is just well-hidden in the wilderness above us. Keep your eyes open when traversing our mountains.

2
Weird Photos

Here is something you do not see every day. In 1995, a horse and rider tumbled down the side of a ravine in Little Tujunga Canyon and the horse became trapped. The Montrose Search and Rescue Team devised a harness for the horse and lifted it out with a helicopter. (*Montrose Search and Rescue*)

Local historians puzzled over this photo for years. It almost looks like a way of hiding illegal alcohol, a common practice in Prohibition-era Crescenta Valley. It was discovered that an ancient bridge across the Verdugo Creek was being propped up by castoff wine barrels. That bridge, obviously rebuilt, is at Shirleyjean Street and La Crescenta Avenue. The year is about 1950. (*Glendale History Room, Library, Arts & Culture Dept., Glendale, CA*)

Police had it easy in the 1930s when roadside signs directed them to crime scenes (only joking). Actually, in 1934, a millionaire was kidnapped and held in a rented house in La Crescenta. The Gettle kidnapping made national news, and when it was over, the property owner made a few bucks letting tourists tour the crime scene, and this sign on Foothill directed them there. (*Glendale History Room, Library, Arts & Culture Dept., Glendale, CA*)

This photo of street violence occurred on Honolulu Avenue, and the thugs shown are Montrose merchants. Seriously though, in the late 1940s, the "Western Days" celebration was held in Montrose. Part of that celebration was a beard-growing contest. Those who would not participate were ceremoniously lassoed and dunked in a bathtub, as seen here. The culmination of the celebration was a rodeo, in which Montrose store owners were pitted against professional rodeo cowboys. Obviously, hilarity ensued. (*Glendale History Room, Library, Arts & Culture Dept., Glendale, CA*)

Illegal liquor stills and smuggling, along with a few "speakeasies" were rampant in CV during Prohibition in the 1920s. Here the local law dumps seized alcohol into the gutter of Ocean View Boulevard in Montrose. Behind them is the Montrose Sheriff Station. Today that building is *Je t'adore* Pet Salon. Note the guy in the photo smoking a cigarette. It is lucky he did not accidently light things off. (*Glendale History Room, Library, Arts & Culture Dept., Glendale, CA*)

In the early 1960s, a car coming down La Crescenta Avenue lost its brakes and sheared off the fire hydrant just above Foothill Boulevard. Bystanders were concerned that the resulting 100-foot geyser would damage the power lines above, so this helpful young man backed his car over the gushing water. The water pressure lifted his car and he was trapped inside until the water was turned off. (*Historical Society of the Crescenta Valley*)

In November 1933, a massive wildfire burned down through Dunsmore Canyon. It burned the huge vineyards of the LeMesnager family and their stone barn, shown here. The barn was filled with big wooden vats of wine, almost ready to bottle for the end of Prohibition. The dark stain on the ground in front of the barn is where thousands of gallons of red wine poured out when the wooden vats burst. Today, the barn has been restored as a nature center at Deukmejian Wilderness Park, and the stained ground is ironically the location of a demonstration vineyard. (*Historical Society of the Crescenta Valley*)

"Botts' dots," so named for the CalTrans engineer who invented them, are reflective ceramic bumps that mark the edges of freeway lanes. In 1978, CalTrans workers applied botts' dots to the 2 Freeway, using go carts—looks like fun. (*Glendale History Room, Library, Arts & Culture Dept., Glendale, CA*)

The high, swooping interchange between the eastbound 134 and the northbound 2 Freeway is a spectacular road to drive today. It was even more spectacular to drive in the mid-seventies before it was completed. (*Glendale History Room, Library, Arts & Culture Dept., Glendale, CA*)

Here is another thing you do not see every day—a camel being led through a bowling alley. The bowling alley is the Verdugo Hills Bowl, which had closed a couple years before this Matchbox 20 music video for "Real World" was filmed in 1998. The alley was torn down soon after, and the Vons supermarket of Foothill Boulevard occupies this site today. (*YouTube*)

This is a huge bust of Paul Von Hindenburg, the president of Germany in the early 1930s. It sat at the southern end of Hindenburg Park, a private park owned by a German cultural group. The men in front are officers from a German warship that visited Los Angeles Harbor before WWII. In 1957, the park was sold to the county and is now the western side of Crescenta Valley Community Regional Park. No one seems to know what happened to the giant head. (*Historical Society of the Crescenta Valley*)

This fuzzy shot is a poor screen capture from a video that went viral worldwide in 2017. The video is clearer and shows what appears to be an ape-like creature swinging though the trees in the Verdugo Mountains near the bottom of Lowell Avenue. There was much speculation that it was a pet chimp that had escaped, but no creature was ever located. (*YouTube*)

This house was not paying attention as it went down the street, and accidently ran into this telephone pole. Actually, during the midnight New Year's Eve Flood of 1934, this house was swept off its foundations. The intact house floated down Del Mar Avenue, crossed Montrose Avenue, and fetched up against this telephone pole. That is Holy Redeemer Church in the background. (*Historical Society of the Crescenta Valley*)

3
Weird People

A "Wild" Apache Girl Grew Up in A Tujunga Castle

One of the last "wild" Apache Native Americans grew up in Tujunga in the 1930s and '40s. This Apache lived in Weatherwolde Castle, the historic faux-castle that was saved from the wrecking ball and restored a few years ago.

The story begins with the last surrender of Geronimo's band of Apaches in 1886. Some of them refused to ever surrender and retreated into the mountains of southern New Mexico, drifting south into Mexico. They continued their war-like ways well into the twentieth century, raiding ranches and retreating back into the Sierra Madre Mountains. The drifting bands were hunted by vengeful Mexicans and slaughtered when they were found. There are legends even today that free Apaches still roam those wild mountains.

In 1932, Jack Harris, an adventurer, and his wife, Dixie, were in Mexico attending to a cattle ranch they co-owned. In the town they were in, Nacori Chico, a band of Mexican cowboys came back from a raid on an Apache camp, dragging three captured Apache children with them. It had been a village of just women and children, and the men had killed the women and burned their homes. Dixie saw that the men were now drunk and intended to kill the children. She confronted the men, grabbed the children, then barricaded herself in her room until they sobered up. Dixie and Jack took two of the terrified children to a convent, but Dixie fell in love with the three-year-old girl named "Bui" (Owl Eyes), and took her back home to the U.S., and eventually to Tujunga, to the Norman-style Weatherwolde Castle they had just bought.

There are several versions of this story. The French researcher Giovanni-Michel Del Franco, who has written extensively on Bui, says the story is not as dramatic as this. His research has shown that a Mexican cowboy searching for a lost cow came upon the Apache encampment. He killed the grandmother and took Bui as a captive. He came back to the Harris's, where Dixie, believing herself to be infertile, decided to adopt the child. Yet like so many ironic adoption stories, Dixie was then able to conceive naturally and the couple returned to the U.S. for the birth of their daughter Ann. The many stories around this are wildly varying because of faulty memories and lack of documentation.

Anyway, they renamed Bui "Carmela," and at first, she remained terrified. She remembered the massacre well, and in her life before that, she was always hiding, always on the run. As she warmed to her adoptive and loving parents and sister, she related her memories. She remembered that she did not know her mother or father, only a grandmother who raised her. The grandmother was a harsh, stern woman, and their survival was predicated on silence. Carmela remembered that there was one child in the band who was too loud, always crying, and Carmela remembered that the grandmother strangled the child. Carmela remembered the gunshots of the Mexican ambushers, seeing her grandmother dead, and the fire afterwards. She was afraid of Hispanics all her life. When she was captured, she was dressed in a primitive buckskin dress and moccasins, and her possessions included some beads and a deck of leather cards, like tarot cards.

When she went to school in largely white Tujunga, she stood out, with her jet-black hair and her starkly Indian features—dark skin, high broad cheekbones, and almond-shaped eyes whose gaze held an incredible bright intensity. She made fast

This portrait of Bui as a child was painted by François Pinna. (*Giovanni-Michel Del Franco*)

friends with an Italian girl, perhaps the only other kid in the neighborhood who was not blonde. When the neighborhood kids played "cowboys and Indians," Carmela was of course always cast as the loser. Only she knew the harsh realty behind their games. Although she had opportunities, she never wanted to go back and talk to other Apaches, or find the other two children that she had been captured with.

Carmela grew into a beautiful young woman and graduated from Verdugo Hills High School. Yet she never married and remained with Dixie in the castle. By the mid-1970s, Jack had died, and Dixie and Carmela moved to Italy, to an ancient stone farmhouse in the Umbrian countryside. From there, the pair travelled extensively in Europe. Oddly, Carmela felt at home in Europe. She told others that her move there felt preordained. She took up photography and immersed herself in European history, forgetting her own. She was completely happy. Again Giovanni-Michel Del Franco disputes this and says Carmela was not happy in Europe, that this was just a "and she lived happily ever after" affectation to the popular story. She died accidently a few years later. She fainted and hit her head in just the wrong place, dying immediately. She is buried in Italy.

So goes the tale of perhaps the last "wild" Apache, who grew up in Tujunga and lived most of her life in a castle, and finished her life in Italy—a remarkable life, from wild Indian to cultured European, via our own Tujunga.

The French researcher and author Giovanni-Michel Del Franco, who specializes in American Indians has written two books on Bui, one a biography: *Je m'appelais Bui*, and a novel, *She Dizhé (Petite Sœur)*. They are available on Amazon but have only been published in the French language.

C.V.'s Civil War Veterans Who Were Not Veterans at All

There are two prominent C.V. pioneers who did not fight in the Civil War, but local legend claims they did. Either they were mistakenly thought of as Civil War veterans, or they lied about their service. We do not really know. Local historian Jo Anne Sadler has written two books about the early C.V. pioneers: *Frontier Days in Crescenta Valley* and *Crescenta Valley Pioneers*, and she delves into this mystery.

We tend to think that everyone in the 1860s fought in the Civil War, but some people did avoid serving. La Crescenta's founder Benjamin Briggs was strongly opposed to the war and moved to California to avoid it. But California was also a place one could re-invent themselves. In the pre-internet world, it was hard to look up facts. If it was advantageous that people thought you were a veteran, what was the harm in not correcting them?

Shields Street and Canyon are named for General John Shields. Two C.V. pioneers wrote about "General" Shields. One of them wrote: "How well I remember General Shields, straight as an arrow, riding horseback through the valley." Another wrote: "He was a retired Confederate Army General and came here for the benefit of his health ... General Shields, while living here, always wore a plug hat and carried a gold-headed cane. He drove fast horses." Shields was a community leader and so was in the newspapers often, almost always referred to as "General." For example, an article from the *L.A. Herald* in 1892 states: "Gen. John H. Shields of La Crescenta was admitted to practice law. General Shields graduated in the law department of the Cincinnati College."

The problem is, there was no Confederate General Shields. As Jo Anne Sadler points out, the Civil War was very well documented and there definitely was no General Shields. There was a Lieutenant Shields, but that was not the same man who we had living in California. According to Sadler's research, La Crescenta's John Shields lived in Tennessee during the war years, already married and with three kids. He did not enlist. He came west with his family in 1874.

So, what was the deal? Was "General" some kind of honorific title? Was it a joke? Where did the Confederate General story come from? There is no evidence he made up anything himself, and yet everyone called him "General." We just do not know.

Colonel Theodor Pickens is considered to be the first permanent American settler in the valley, settling here on Briggs Terrace in 1871. He was referred to as "Colonel" Pickens in the 1950s by Charles Pate. Pate came to the valley in 1893 and so would have overlapped in the time Pickens was here. Pate claimed in his memoirs, written as an old man, that Pickens had been a colonel in the Union Army. He further wrote that Pickens had left Kentucky to fight for the Union and was wounded in the wrist. This has been accepted as fact ever since.

Again, Jo Anne Sadler's research showed no such person was ever in the Union Army. Our Pickens was indeed from Kentucky, born there in 1842. He would have been the right age for the war, but well-documented records verify that he never joined. By 1870, he had come west.

Unlike General Shields, no one other than Pate ever called him "Colonel." The use of colonel was a common way to give respect to someone back then, to indicate an aristocratic background, usually from the South (like Colonel Sanders, for example). Maybe he was introduced to Pate as Colonel Pickens and the story grew from there. Maybe Pate, who had come from England, did not understand that.

Whatever the case, these are two C.V. pioneers who were, and often still are, mistakenly thought to be Civil War veterans. We will probably never know if it was a purposeful lie, a case of mistaken identity, or a joke.

Hollywood's King of Sleaze Lived in La Crescenta

Most everyone has heard of Ed Woods, creator of the film *Plan 9 From Outer Space*. He was immortalized in the Tim Burton movie *Ed Woods* as having made the worst Hollywood movies ever. But his title as worst filmmaker pales when compared to the lesser-known 1930s career of Crescenta Valley resident Dwain Esper. He is considered to be the "Father of the Exploitation Film," and he produced an astounding array of terribly made "shocker" films about sex, drugs, and violence during his fifteen years in La Crescenta.

Esper lived in what we today know as the Bishop Estate, which in 1966 was seized by eminent domain to become Mountain Avenue Elementary School. The grand mansion on 5 landscaped acres was built in 1923, but in 1929, it was bought by Dwain and Hildegarde Esper, who moved in with their two young kids. Dwain Esper was a smooth-talking conman, who, after working as a motorcycle stuntman, had made a fortune as a contractor in the 1920s. Hildegarde had grown up a "carny," following her drug-addicted uncle through the sideshow circuit, and being displayed nude to attract a crowd. Dwain and Hildegarde both had sleazy pasts.

Dwain was said to be one of the best conmen ever and often conned people out of money at dinner parties staged at his La Crescenta mansion. In 1930, Dwain foreclosed on a loan and obtained a small film production studio in Hollywood. He realized he could make a fortune making "shocker" films featuring nudity and debauchery, distributing them himself, outside the bounds of Hollywood's Hays Code, which would have banned movies like his.

So, a sort of twisted La Crescenta "Mom and Pop" business was run out of the Esper's home on Mountain Avenue. They formed a company called "Road Show Attractions." Hildegarde wrote the scripts. Dwain made the horrible movies, sometimes directing, sometimes producing, sometimes merely taking an existing movie and inserting "nudie" clips to make the movie more salacious. Dwain and Hildegarde occasionally acted in them. Then they would take their film on the road.

Dwain, along with hired men, barnstormed the Midwest and South, renting out movie houses and burlesque theaters, even setting up tents. They plastered the little towns with posters that trumpeted "Adults Only." They came up with gimmicky items to display in the lobby such as John Dillinger's gun or the famous mummified body of bandit Elmer McCurdy (who eventually ended his traveling career at the Pike funhouse in Long Beach). The shows were often promoted as educational, and Hildegarde would accompany the movie with a lecture about the dangers of drugs and sex.

But the films were the real star. Here are just a few. *Sins of Love* was a cautionary tale about venereal disease. *Narcotic* was a cautionary tale of drug addiction, which incongruously featured footage of a Caesarian birth. A heroin-addicted medical student is reduced to selling drugs in a carnival side-show. Hildegarde wrote the script based on her own experiences working side-shows with her addicted uncle.

There was nothing cautionary about *Sex Maniac*; this was simply made to shock. It featured mad doctors, zombies, rape, murder, insanity, and animal cruelty. This movie is cited by several film critics as the worst movie ever made, but to be fair, it did come with a lecture by Hildegarde, as advertised: "Hear dynamic sex lectures! Plain facts about secret sin!"

Another was *Marijuana: The Weed with Roots in Hell*—the title tells it all.

Two other instructional films were *How to Take a Bath* and *How to Undress in Front of Your Husband*; the latter was remarkable in that it starred two minor female movie stars, one of them Mrs. John Barrymore. Techniques for undressing as seen through the eyes of a peeping Tom.

Dwain Esper also reissued existing films, popularizing them with his own brand of showmanship. *Reefer Madness* and *Freaks* were two, which, thanks to him, remain cult classics today.

Straight outta La Crescenta—this is the movie poster for *Marijuana: The Weed with Roots in Hell*, an exploitation film written and produced where Mountain Avenue Elementary School is today. (*Wikipedia*)

From 1929 until 1944, when the Bishop family moved in, La Crescenta was home to the king and queen of sleaze. An unusual family for quiet La Crescenta, and an unusual legacy for the Mountain Avenue School site.

La Crescenta's Connection to *I Love Lucy*

This story comes to us from the late Charles Bausback, who was an institution here in the valley. He was a fabulous storyteller, and he had a photographic memory of the past. Some of his stories seemed far-fetched, but over the years, many of the stories that seemed to be "tall tales" were borne out as true. This is one of those tales. His stories were as long as they were entertaining, so this is a shortened version.

The story of the *I Love Lucy* TV show and her on-screen pregnancy was an interesting one. As many of us know, Lucille Ball and Desi Arnez played a married couple (Lucy and Ricky Ricardo) on the wildly popular sitcom in the early 1950s, but they were married in real life as well. At that time, any implication of sex on TV was strictly forbidden, including pregnancy. When Lucille Ball became pregnant during the filming of the show, it was assumed that she would step away from filming. But Lucy and Desi were at the height of their popularity, filmed in their own studio—Desilu Studios—and they wielded some power. They made the decision to buck the system and make Lucy's pregnancy (and the birth of Desi Arnez, Jr., in 1953) a part of the show. The boy, called "Little Ricky," was a central part of *I Love Lucy* through the years, but was played by various child actors, not the real Desi, Jr.

Getting back to La Crescenta, there used to be a small neighborhood grocery store on Florencita Avenue just below Montrose Avenue. It is a house today, 2460 Florencita, but last time I checked, you could still make out that it used to be a market. It was run in the 1950s by a local guy named Max Mayer. Max was a character. For instance, he ran two telegraph services from the store: Western Union and Postal Telegraph and he kept his "official hats" for each service in the back room. If you wanted to send a Western Union telegraph, he would excuse himself, disappear into the back room, and reappear wearing the Western Union hat to take your order.

According to Charles Bausback, in 1953, Max Mayer and his wife gave birth to twin boys on the exact same day and in the exact same hospital as Lucille Ball was giving birth to Desi, Jr. When the *I Love Lucy* producers came to visit Lucy and Desi, Jr., they looked through the window of the nursery, saw Lucy's baby, and right next to him the two Mayer twin boys looking very much like Lucy's baby.

In those days, a child actor was not allowed to be under hot studio lights for very long. Twins were often recruited to play a single child, with the twins to be switched out for one another under the lights. Again, according to Charles, Max Mayer was contacted by the producers to see if his boys could be hired to play "Little Ricky," and he said yes. The twins—Joe and Mike Mayer—were used to play "Little Ricky" for about three years. With the money the Mayers received, Max was able to go to college and finish his degree.

That is Charles' story, and he is sticking to it. A quick check of the internet says the Simmons twins were the first Little Ricky, soon replaced by the Mayer twins. They had been spotted at a "twins picnic" and recruited to play the part. They did very well in the role, but after three seasons, their parents declined to continue. After that, child actor Richard Thibodeaux (stage name Richard Keith) took on the role. The Mayer twins grew up in C.V., graduated from Crescenta Valley High, and went on to college. Today, they both live in Idaho.

For a historian, it is sometimes hard to separate fact from fiction, and in some cases, not worth the effort. The Mayer twins did play Little Ricky and they were from La Crescenta. On the details, it is Charles *v.* the internet—we will go with Charles.

The Woman in the Iron Lung

One vivid memory of the author's time at La Crescenta Elementary School was waiting to cross the street to the school on the corner of La Crescenta and Prospect. We kids would surreptitiously glance across Prospect to the bay window of the house on the corner. Quite often, we would see a mirror projecting a woman's face, and it always seemed she was looking right at us. We kids had heard there was this lady in an iron lung, whatever that was, and that she never left the house. Over the years since, I have learned what an iron lung was, and that that woman had lived in the device for thirty-seven years, longer than any other patient (at that time). Here is her story.

After WWII, polio seemed to be everywhere. Papers would report outbreaks on the front page, and suspected areas of transmission—such as movie theaters and public pools—would be shut down in response to public fear. In 1948, Laurel Nesbitt was a busy young mother of two in La Crescenta when she experienced a week of flu-like symptoms that developed into muscular problems. When she could no longer move on her own, she was taken to County Hospital, already overflowing with polio victims. She lay on the floor of the hallway, gasping for breath. When she was finally slipped into an iron lung, she was initially relieved, finally able to catch her breath. But three weeks turned into three months, and after three years in the hospital it became obvious that her body would never breathe on its own and the doctors sent her home, permanently trapped inside the lung.

The iron lung was set up in their living room, a big steel cylinder like an oversized water heater. Laurel's head stuck out one end, an airtight seal tight around her collarbone. Every four seconds, the cylinder would de-pressurize and pressurize, causing her chest to expand (forcing a breath in through her exposed nose) and contract (pushing the breath back out). From the neck up, she was normal, and although flat on her back, she had a set of mirrors with which she could see the world, including kids going to and from the school across the street.

Despite her devastating disability, Laura kept an optimistic outlook on life and successfully raised her two kids. She was quite social and was able to talk on the phone. Often, strangers hearing of her plight would stop in to visit. All who knew her said that as amazing as she was, her husband Don was even more so. He was a saint, providing for all her needs.

In 1965, she became a Jehovah's Witness and found renewed purpose in life. She spent hours on the phone, talking to those in need of spiritual guidance or prayer, and meeting with Jehovah's Witnesses from all over the world. She also became a major fundraiser for polio research. Her life was very full.

In 1985, at the age of seventy-two, she faced emergency surgery. Her doctor insisted that she would need a transfusion in order to survive the operation, but she was adamant to her faith—Jehovah's Witnesses could absolutely not receive blood or organ donations. She told the doctor that she would not tolerate being transfused.

The four-hour operation, with no transfusion, was only partially successful. When she awoke, she was in a hospital bed, outside her iron lung for the first time in thirty-seven years. The doctors had routed a portable respirator into her lungs through a tracheotomy. The new form of breathing caused her panic, and she felt once again that

The iron lung was a chilling sight during the polio epidemics of the 1940s and '50s. Note the mirror that allowed the iron lung's occupant to see the world. It was this kind of mirror projecting Laurel Nesbitt's face that us kids saw in her front window. (*University of Rochester*)

she could not catch her breath. As well, the tracheotomy prevented her from speaking. She died only three days later.

Through research for this piece, some surprising facts were learned about polio. Although we do not see it here, in other parts of the world, polio is alive and well, and sadly there still is no cure. The Rotary Club has dedicated their organization to wiping out polio, and have had good success. Support the Rotarians and polio research so that sad stories like Laura Nesbitt's will stop replaying.

In Big Tujunga Canyon, a long-haired Eden Ahbez sits next to an outdoor oven that he used to make food while living in the wilderness during the 1950s and 1960s. The remains of this oven are still there. (*Joe Romersa/Shadowbox Studio*)

"Nature Boy" Lived in Big Tujunga Canyon

"There was a boy, a very strange enchanted boy ..." These were the opening lines of Nat King Cole's hit song "Nature Boy." The song was a semi-autobiographical piece written by the famous Los Angeles pre-hippie icon Eden Ahbez, whose main home (campsite really) was in Big Tujunga Canyon.

Eden was born in the slums of New York in 1908 as George Alexander Aberle (Eden Ahbez was a name he adopted in the early 1940s). He grew up in an orphanage, but was adopted as a teenager by a family in Kansas. In the 1930s, he developed his musical talent in Kansas City and New York. He joined the thousands of jobless men who lived in vagabond style, crisscrossing the country by rail, thumb, and foot. During this period, he read up on Eastern philosophy and the nutritional benefits of natural foods.

In 1941, he landed in L.A. and got a job playing piano in a health food restaurant called Eutropheon on Laurel Canyon Boulevard. Eutropheon was one of the centers of the pre-hippie lifestyle of that era that promoted primitive living and raw foods. L.A. had since the 1880s been a center of the health food movement. We had a health food store in Montrose in the 1920s. Eden was influenced by the owners of the restaurant, natural-lifestyle pioneers John and Vera Richter. Eden and others associated with the restaurant adopted Eastern philosophies, grew their hair and beards, wore robes, and camped outdoors, eating only raw foods (the famous Gypsy Boots was one of this group). They were dubbed "the California Nature Boys."

The years just after the war found Eden regularly camping with his new wife Anna in Big Tujunga Canyon. Old-timers place that site as being between the modern-day Little League field and the detention camp. In 1947, Eden penned "Nature Boy" and tried to get the sheet music to the moderately successful Nat King Cole, then playing in a Los Angeles theater. The long-haired oddball was ignored, but he left the music with Cole's assistant. Later, when Cole read the music, he was taken with its haunting melody and tried the song out to live audiences with great success. Cole wanted to record the song, but needed to get the rights from Eden who had disappeared back into his temporary campsites around L.A. Legend says that Cole finally tracked him down camped under the Hollywood sign. The song was a number one hit for Cole and introduced him to a wider audience, cementing his fame.

As a result of Cole's hit, Eden became a celebrity, and his then odd lifestyle became a focus of a fascinated America. The term "nature boy" became a part of our language and culture. Photos of him, his wife, and his son preparing raw foods or playing bongo drums in Big Tujunga Canyon were widely viewed. Characters based on "Nature Boy" popped up in movies, pro-wrestling, Bugs Bunny cartoons, and comic books. As a result of his fame, other musicians and songwriters flocked to Eden. He churned out a string of minor hits for Doris Day, Frank Sinatra, Eartha Kitt, and many others. His songwriting ranged from the easy-listening style of "Nature Boy" to jazz, rock 'n' roll, and country western. He even collaborated (un-credited) with songwriter Stan Jones on the cowboy classic "Ghost Riders in the Sky."

All this time, he was camping outdoors in various sites ranging from Silver Lake and Whittier to Joshua Tree and Indio, but returning often to Big Tujunga. In the 1950s and '60s, American culture caught up with Eden, first with the beatnik movement, then with the hippie movement. Life's tragedies caught up with him as well as his wife died in 1965 of leukemia, followed by his son in 1971 in a drowning accident. Eden himself died in a car crash in 1995.

Eden Ahbez's physical life was filled with pain and tragedy, but his mind and spirit existed above it all, always promoting a message of peace and tranquility. As the song says, "The greatest thing you'll ever learn, is just to love and be loved in return."

The Utopia at the Top of La Crescenta Avenue

A *Crescenta Valley Ledger* article from January 1945 reads: "New Life Center Officially Opens, Public Programs Scheduled Soon." The article detailed the sale of the former Harvey Bissell property to the New Life Foundation.

The Bissell property, which is now the Pinecrest neighborhood at the top of La Crescenta Avenue, has a long and interesting history. One of the very early ranches in the valley, it was above the property developed into La Crescenta by Dr. Benjamin Briggs. It had been owned in the 1880s by John Shields, for which Shields Canyon was named, and then by Col. Samuel Merrill, a high-ranking diplomat and friend to President Benjamin Harrison. He appropriately named the ranch Granite Heights. In the 1910s, the property was purchased by Harvey Bissell, of the Bissell Vacuum Cleaner family. He renamed the property the "Hi-up Ranch" and built a veritable paradise as his personal playground, with groves of trees and gardens, walking paths, and stables for his thoroughbred horses.

By the 1940s, the property was for sale again, and the article detailed its purchase by the New Life Foundation and the group's plans for the property's future. The New Life Foundation was an offshoot of the teachings of one of the many Indian mystics that traveled to Los Angeles in the early 1900s to establish religious centers. This particular one was Avatar Meher Baba, and several of his centers still exist worldwide today.

The New Life Center of La Crescenta was the brainchild of a Hollywood screenwriter, Alexander Markey. He was quite a character—a member of the Explorer's Club, world traveler, chronicler of New Zealand's Maori culture, and an advocate of the "natural way of life." He was joined in his plans by an impressive list of thinkers and artists. Some of the names, immediately recognizable in the 1940s but obscure today, were Dr. Fritz Kunkel, a world-famous psychologist; author Jean Adriel; educator Dr. Hugh Teetzel; and actors Helen Freeman and Beulah Bondi (who played Jimmy Stewart's mom in both *Mr. Smith Goes to Washington* and *It's A Wonderful Life*).

The former Bissell property was described as a "heaven on earth," with lush gardens, interesting and plentiful wildlife, and (most important in C.V.) its own water supply from a crystal pure spring.

The New Life Center was to be a cultural and humanitarian center, but it also would be used as a rehabilitation resort for both returning war veterans and underprivileged gifted children. Admittance to the resort was to be based entirely on the individual's needs, and qualifications were to be determined without economic or class distinction, with all races, religions, and nationalities welcome. Several dwellings for guests were planned, and only those with "ideals of unselfish service to man" would be invited to live there. Art studios and craft workshops were planned to be built, small "health farms" would be carved out, and the center would operate its own radio station.

Some of the most ambitious plans outlined in the article involved two large theaters to be developed on the property—for example, a 500-seat indoor theater would be built inside the Bissell's huge former horse barn, as well as a 1,200-seat outdoor Greek theater. Both theaters would be planned and guided by Hollywood writers, actors, and directors for year-round performances of devotional and humanitarian productions.

The article finishes by saying that Dr. Kunkel would be celebrating the purchase of the property by kicking off a series of lectures for the community to be held at the center. The first of the Sunday lectures would be "Character Problems and Their Solutions."

However, this utopian paradise seems to have been a flash in the pan. Soon after the establishment of the La Crescenta retreat, Meher Baba, the leader of the sect, perhaps sensing that the area was destined to grow quickly, asked his New Life Center followers to find another site further from L.A. They sold the La Crescenta property and purchased a 173-acre site in Ojai. Ojai's Meher Mount is still thriving today.

Meher Baba has a fascinating story. The Indian mystic took a vow of silence in 1925 and communicated with his followers using an alphabet board and hand gestures. He required nothing of his followers—no money, no rites or rituals, only a focus on God and His love. He traveled extensively and attracted followers worldwide. He found fertile ground in L.A. in the 1930s and was a big sensation with the Hollywood crowd, including Charles Laughton, Tallulah Bankhead, Boris Karloff, Douglas Fairbanks, and Mary Pickford. In the 1960s, he attracted a rock-and-roll following, as several rock stars looked to the east for inspiration.

The Who's Pete Townsend studied Meher Baba's teachings and incorporated him and his message into many of his works. The rock opera *Tommy* is dedicated to Meher Baba; at the end of the famous rock opera, the main character, Tommy, is a spiritual leader who does not speak, just like Meher Baba. Townsend's most famous reference to Meher is the rock anthem "Baba O'Riley," sometimes known as "Teenage Wasteland." Meher Baba had a strong anti-drug message in his teachings, and Pete Townsend was moved by those teachings during the Who's performance at Woodstock. Townsend looked out at a crowd wasted on drugs ("It's only teenage wasteland"), seemingly proud of their intoxication ("We're all wasted!"). The violin solo is based on Indian classical music, again a tribute to Meher Baba. "O'Riley" refers to composer Terry Riley, who inspired the synthesizer track on the song.

Another follower of Meher Baba was 1970s songstress Melanie, whose biggest hit "Lay Down (Candles in the Rain)" included the lyrics, "Meher Baba lives again, Candles in the rain." However, my favorite Meher song reference comes from the 1980s. During those years, followers of Meher used to hand out cards featuring a photo of Meher Baba grinning happily, and a small two-line quote that summed up his message. One of these cards fell into the hands of an unknown vocalist, who incorporated the quote into a song, and in 1988, Bobby McFerrin hit it big with Meher's message: "Don't worry—Be happy."

So we can imagine what could have been had the La Crescenta property stayed in the hands of Mejer Baba. Perhaps a benefit concert in the 1970s by The Who at the New Life Center in La Crescenta? But that was not to be. As we know, the property was later developed by Webster Wiley into the beautiful terraced Pinecrest housing.

The Rainmaker Visits La Crescenta

A few years ago, a local historian discovered and wrote the story of a local visit by one of the most famous "rainmakers" of the early twentieth century. In Jo Ann Sadler's book *Frontier Days in Crescenta Valley*, she writes of Professor Charles Hatfield's time in La Crescenta attempting to make it rain in August 1904.

Professor Charles Hatfield, like many of the so-called "Professors" of that era, was not really a professor. He was a high school drop-out who sold and repaired sewing machines, but in his spare time, he studied climate research, particularly the pseudo-science of rainmaking. He had moved to Glendale with his brother Paul, and by 1902, he had settled on his own blend of twenty-three different chemicals that would produce rain when ignited on top of a high tower.

His first experiments were in November 1902 in Big Tujunga Canyon. According to his own records, that experiment resulted in 3 inches of rain for the foothills. He took his first paying rainmaking job in the summer of 1904. A group of Los Angeles farmers pledged $50 to Hatfield if he could make it rain. Despite Hatfield's earlier experiment, L.A. had still been experiencing a drought.

Professor Hatfield drove his wagon up from Glendale to the Crescenta Valley. He followed Verdugo Road up to the brushy area that would be Montrose a decade later. He turned left onto Honolulu, a rough dirt track through the sagebrush. Hatfield followed it and chose a spot at the base of New York Avenue for his operation. Today, that would be the far east side of Crescenta Valley Park. Hatfield and his brother Paul erected a 20-foot-tall derrick, topped with a 10-foot-wide platform. On the platform, they set up what appeared to be a smokestack, and next to it a rain gauge. Below the tower, they set up a tent to live in and to mix their chemicals.

What exactly Hatfield did with the chemicals is lost to time, but for a week, the professor, clad in a business suit, stood atop the platform, busily working for hours at a time, burning his noxious mixtures. His younger brother Paul, who served as his assistant, scurried up and down a ladder from the tent to the platform and back again, carrying loads of chemicals, and tending to the camp and horses.

An elderly Englishman named Metcalf who had a bee-keeping operation nearby tried to be neighborly and chat with the odd pair, but they were too busy and shooed him away. He was curious what they were up to. Later, the professor and Paul took a much-needed break and strolled away from camp. Metcalf stole into their tent, but they returned and caught him there. Even though he protested that he was just there to say hello, this time they ran Metcalf off at the point of a shotgun. Metcalf later reported his encounter to the *L.A. Times*, helping them write a satirical account of the rainmaker.

But it did indeed rain. The L.A. farmers were so impressed, they paid Professor Hatfield $100 instead of the agreed on $50. The professor's fame spread, and he began to charge bigger bounties for rain all through California and even to Alaska, although he was not always able to deliver.

His biggest hit was in San Diego in the winter of 1915–16. The City Council agreed to pay him $10,000 to fill a newly built reservoir. In December, he started his rainmaking operation, and in January, rain of Biblical proportions came down. Two dams overflowed and the area was inundated. Twenty deaths occurred from the flooding. The angry City Council reneged on the deal, instead trying unsuccessfully to pin millions of dollars in property damage on the professor.

Professor Hatfield continued his rainmaking magic for several decades. He died in 1958 and never revealed his formula. A bit of trivia: The 1957 Burt Lancaster film *The Rainmaker* is very loosely based on Hatfield.

Meteorologists today discredit his ability to create rain. They instead cite that he had knowingly conducted his rainmaking operations at times that rain was likely. Whatever the case, Professor Hatfield, rainmaker, had established his reputation in 1904, right here in La Crescenta.

4
Weird Places

The Lost Canyon Community of Aztec Park

For years now, there have been rumors about abandoned cabins and foundations way up high in Haines Canyon, just over the border of Tujunga. Photos exist of extensive foundation work half hidden by brush. Apparently, this was the tiny community of Aztec Park.

In the 1880s, when La Crescenta and Tujunga were first being settled, those early residents staked out their homes close to what little water flowed into the valleys. In La Crescenta, Theodor Pickens and Benjamin Briggs located themselves on the stream of Pickens Canyon, while in Tujunga, the small community of Glorietta Heights formed on the stream coming from Haines Canyon. Early settler Phil Begue claimed the water rights in the canyon and built a dam and reservoir that watered the orchards and vineyards below. The Begue family and others built little cabins along the stream higher up in Haines Canyon.

Later, in the 1920s, the Haines Canyon Water Company bougt the water rights and developed an extensive water system for the growing community of Tujunga. As well, a gravel quarry was opened in the canyon, and it is said that workers for that and the water company had cabins there. This cluster of cabins, along with the ones built earlier, was apparently called Aztec Park.

All that remains today are clues. A 1933 topo map shows several roads in upper Haines Canyon. The map indicates ten structures along these roads. A very old road sign in the Little Landers Historical Society's museum points the way to "Aztec Park—2 miles." Even the modern online Google satellite view names a trail in the upper reaches of Haines Canyon "Azteca Spur."

The author has collected snippets of memories from old-timers. "Phil Begue and his father had a cabin or camp in Haines Canyon as did some of the other East Glorietta Heights early timers. That was in the late 1800s when these folks built their cabins up there."

"I think the dam keeper and water company people lived up there."

"At Aztec Park in Haines Canyon the foundations of some cottages were damaged as a result of the 13 inches of rain that fell in one seven-day period [in 1921]. The minimum damage sustained was due to the efficiency of the check dams that were installed in 1914."

"The only thing I heard from my parents was that the late '30s flood washed away cabins."

"In the early 1960s there were remnants of the old Haines Canyon water company still there. Part way up the canyon was an abandoned cabin with a very old rusty car parked next to it. The brush fire in 1975 destroyed all this."

I had heard that a group of mountain bikers had cleared some of the foundations, so I hiked up to view the area. It is an easy couple-mile hike up Haines Canyon. At a certain point, the main trail leaves the canyon and heads up toward Mt. Lukens, but I kept to the trail to the left, following the canyon, and walked on an engineered mountain bike course, with banked curves and jumps. About 500 yards up from there, one can see the cleared area, marked by much stonework, on the north side of the canyon. I actually followed the overgrown remains of an old asphalt road toward the cleared area.

The foundations are huge, consisting of seven or eight large oak-shaded terraces. Tall stone retaining walls front each terrace and stone steps allow access to the level above. It looks much like a huge terraced yard, where there may have been orchards at one time. Stone walls wind off into the underbrush, promising more mysterious stonework. Kudos to the mountain bikers that cleared this area of overgrowth. It must have been a huge job.

There must be more foundations like this in the heavy overgrowth of this canyon. No doubt a future brush fire will reveal more. In the meantime, we are left guessing about the true size and history of the lost community of Aztec Park.

These extensive rock walls and steps far back in the wilderness of Haines Canyon are the remains of the lost community of Aztec Park. These ruins were exposed thanks to backbreaking work by a group of mountain bikers. Who knows what else is covered by the thick brush surrounding this exposed rock-work? (*Craig Durst*)

The Czechoslovakian Hall of La Crescenta

Slovakian immigrant Henry Biescar, after prospering in Los Angeles around the turn of the century, retired to La Crescenta in 1915. He purchased 11 acres in La Crescenta above Foothill.

The Slovakian community in Los Angeles was vibrant, and several cultural organizations for both Czechs and Slovaks thrived here. In 1928, several L.A.-based Czech and Slovakian groups banded together under the umbrella group the Czechoslovak Patronat. They began the task of raising money to build a hall, and Henry Biescar donated 4 acres in La Crescenta for its site.

By 1933, $10,000 dollars had been raised and construction began on the hall at 2723 Orange Avenue, across the street from where Monte Vista Elementary School is today. The hall was large—65 × 85 feet and two stories. Interior features included a 40 × 60-foot ballroom with a speaking platform, a dining room, a billiards room, and a library. The extensive grounds were landscaped to form a beautiful park for big picnics and outdoor activities. This large-scale construction activity was a financial boon to the depressed economy of La Crescenta as local labor and materials were used for the entire project.

An opening day ceremony was orchestrated, attracting thousands to the event, with representatives from Czechoslovakia in attendance. The hall was wildly popular with the many Czech and Slovak organizations in L.A. and was well-used each weekend for ethnic dances, parties, and picnics. October 28 each year was a huge celebration—Czechoslovakian Independence Day, honoring the formation of an independent Czechoslovakia in 1918. Also called Masaryk Day after Czechoslovakia's first president, the event drew scores of Czech, Slovak, and Bohemian organizations together at the hall in La Crescenta for a weekend of dances in native costume, folk songs, and feasts of old-country food—roast pork, sauerkraut and dumplings, and traditional pastries. The event would attract thousands.

The Czechoslovakian Hall was rented out to other ethnic groups as well. The *L.A. Times* reported that in 1936, hundreds of Poles attended a picnic there, to feast on Polish foods and dance waltzes, all to raise money to build a Polish Hall in Los Angeles. In 1937, a huge Hungarian Festival was held there, sponsored by a Los Angeles-based Hungarian-language newspaper. A Hungarian Gypsy band provided the music for folk dances in native costumes, and film star Bela Lugosi acted as master of ceremonies. For La Crescenta, the park was a boon to the local economy as outside dollars flooded in each weekend. One old-timer told me that as boys, he and his brothers would sneak into the weekly events to score free food and beer.

The parties went on and on at the Czechoslovakian Hall, through the 1930s and into the '40s. However, problems began to crop up as the post-war housing boom took hold in C.V. The hall, originally located out in the sagebrush, was now surrounded by suburban homes. By 1948, the weekend parties—with hundreds of cars, loud music, and lots of drinking—began to grate on the new neighbors of the Czechoslovakian Hall. The surrounding homeowners presented a petition to County Regional Planning asking them to exert some control over the events staged at the hall. Planning ruled that the owners of the hall, the Czechoslovakian Patronat, could no longer rent the hall to outside organizations. At the same time, the county supervisors, also under pressure from the neighbors, began to pester the Patronat to upgrade the hall, threatening to revoke their license entirely.

Faced with the reduced rental income and added costs to upgrade the hall, the Patronat sold the property. Henry Biescar's son sued the Patronat on the basis that the donated land was donated by his father to be used for the hall and not sold, and won the suit. Today, the Gethsemane Lutheran Church occupies part of that large lot.

The Slovakian–American Biescar family and the short-lived Czechoslovakian Hall is an example of yet another immigrant group that influenced the growth of La Crescenta.

The Watts Towers of La Crescenta

Dunsmore Park, on Dunsmore Avenue above Foothill Boulevard, contains a fascinating example of folk art, very similar to the famed Watts Towers.

On the sloped acreage of the park are miles of decorative retaining walls snaking through the landscaped grounds. The low walls are built of a myriad of materials mortared in place to create a joyful explosion of colors and shapes. The main construction is of stones and chunks of minerals collected from all over the United States. Rocks of green, red, and pink are mixed with the occasional native granite, interspersed with construction rubble, including intact sections of brick wall placed at odd angles. The jumble is artistically punctuated with objects of daily life in the early part of the last century—wagon wheels, farm tools, kitchen utensils, and car parts. Many of the gears, water faucets, forks, and spoons are embedded in slabs of concrete in patterns that create sunbursts and smiley faces.

Some of the objects are rare enough to take center stage on *Antiques Roadshow*, such as an old trolley conductor's ticket punch or an antique beer tap (which would explain why some objects have been pried out over the years, ending up in someone's private collection or on eBay). A stroll through the park is a feast for the imagination.

The history of the park is nearly as fascinating as the walls themselves. Originally carved out of the sagebrush in 1933 as the Mount Lukens Sanitarium, it joined the dozens of other tuberculosis and asthma hospitals that the area was famed for. Its career as an artistic canvas began in 1946 when the sanitarium was purchased by Milton Hofert, a prodigal son whose father ran an L.A. manufacturing company (which today still produces Christmas ornaments).

After some brushes with the law in the 1920s, Hofert joined the Merchant Marine. While traveling the world, he married a foreign bride, but she died in childbirth along with his child. He never remarried. Sometime soon after the war, he bought the sanitarium, although he was not a doctor. Though he had plenty of money from the family fortune, he was known as eccentric and reclusive and was rumored to have stayed on the sanitarium site in a pup tent. He was just sort of odd.

For ten years, Hofert must have given his full attention to creating his artistic walls. It is rumored that he was given prisoners from the Montrose jail for heavy labor, and

This is a small sample of the whimsical "rock and junk art" that is everywhere in Dunsmore Park. It is a feast for the eyes and for the imagination. (*Author*)

perhaps he employed patients from the sanitarium as well. Who ran the sanitarium is anyone's guess—perhaps the "inmates ran the asylum."

By 1956, Glendale was anxious to add more parkland for its recently annexed portion of the Crescenta Valley, and Hofert was ready to move on. Hofert offered the land to the city at a reduced rate if they would agree to preserve his walls. The city wanted no part of that restriction, but a compromise was struck by 1957, and true to Hofert's wishes, the walls have for the most part been preserved. The community room is a remnant of Hofert's sanitarium as well.

Hofert moved to Big Bear, where he continued his penchant for bringing joy to the world. He created Holiday Hill, a winter playground facility for kids. In the late 1990s, when he was nearly 100 years old, he donated Holiday Hill to the city of Big Bear for use as a performing arts center. His name lives on there in several plaques, and in Hofert Hall, an auditorium for the community.

Next time you have a free hour, take a stroll through Dunsmore Park to discover (or re-discover) C.V.'s own version of the Watts Towers.

World Famous Goats of the Crescenta Valley

In the 1920s, the Crescenta Valley was home to several goat farms for the production of goat milk. Goat milk was then, like now, considered to be a health food. Milk goats were a hot item, particularly in the health-conscious Crescenta Valley, where many invalids had moved for the natural restorative powers of our valley. The Silver Spur Goat Farm and Fair Hope Ranch were the names of a couple local goat ranches, but the best-known goat farm was the Rosemont Ranch, under the ownership of a master goat breeder, James Basil McLaughlin.

The story of Rosemont Ranch starts in the late 1800s, when the valley was a favored health retreat and retirement spot for many clergymen and scholars. A retired minister, a Reverend Gordon, decided to make his home in the healthful air of the Crescenta Valley. He chose a 10-acre site above Foothill around today's Orange Avenue, between Briggs and Rosemont Avenues, and named his new place Rosemont. Whether the street is named after his home or *vice versa* is unknown. Gordon had been a missionary in the Middle East and wanted to create a bit of the Holy Land at Rosemont. He had some money from Texas oil wells and used it to plant trees named in the Bible—orange, pomegranate, olive, cedar, and palm, along with a vineyard.

In 1910, lawyer J. B. McLaughlin gained the property in settlement for attorney fees. His wife Dorothy was well-educated and accomplished—a graduate of Vassar and the first librarian of UCLA. The two built a palatial home in the center of the property. It was three stories, the lower part of stone and the rest of wood in a Normandy chateau style, with a peaked tiled roof. It featured wide porches on two floors and spacious rooms. Like many Normandy-style homes, the dominant architectural feature was a tall wide tower on one side of the house, with a circular stairway winding up the center of the tower. The structure stands out prominently in old photos of the valley.

J. B. McLaughlin threw himself into the life of a gentleman farmer, collecting the bountiful harvest of the many fruit trees already on the property, plus raising pure-bred Collie dogs. However, his passion was breeding goats, and by the late 1910s/early 1920s, his Rosemont Ranch dominated the goat world, his particular specialty being Toggenburg Milch goats. The ranch offered pure-bred goats for sale and stud services. The stud services seemed to be Rosemont's main deal, with service prices ranging from $10 up to $25. The stud goats' names were impressive—Michael Angelo, King of the Alps, and Emperor Sigmund. Rosemont's female goats regularly set records for milk production. As a matter of fact, Rosemont Ranch was home to Polly-Mac, the world-record milk producer of that era—15.4 pounds of milk in one day (milk is often measured in weight rather than volume to calibrate for foam and butterfat content). Polly-Mac was named "The World's Best Milk Goat" by the American Goat Society.

According to an article in *Goat World* magazine from 1921, Rosemont Ranch received hundreds of visitors each year to view his prize-winning goats, but McLaughlin's crowning achievement was the sale of one of his goats in 1922 to a millionaire in Chicago. The goat fetched $1,600, which was the highest price ever paid for a single goat. The sale made national news. It is safe to say that back then, goats were a bigger deal than they are today.

Tragedy was visited on the happy life of the McLaughlins when their son, a criminal attorney, was shot dead by a suspect in an L.A. courtroom in 1937. In 1940, the property was bought by Charles and Lillian Brown, who lived there for thirty years until a fire destroyed part of the house; soon after, the 1971 earthquake made the remainder

A dapper-looking J. B. McLaughlin shows off his pride and joy, the world-champion milk goat Polly Mac of the Rosemont Goat Ranch. Goats were a big deal in old La Crescenta. (*Glendale History Room, Library, Arts & Culture Dept., Glendale, CA*)

of the home uninhabitable. The house was demolished and the remaining property was subdivided.

The legacy left behind are scores of posed photos of McLaughlin's prize-winning goats that are part of the historical photos collection of the Glendale Central Library, and Laughlin Street named after J. B. McLaughlin, the master goat man of the Crescenta Valley.

The Hostetter Graphite Mine in the Verdugos

The author has written several times in the past about the legendary "mystery mine" of the Verdugo Mountains. Many remnants of this old mine exist, scattered over the mountainside just south of the 210 Freeway, across from the Verdugo Hills Golf Course. Mine car rails, heavy machinery half-buried in the hillside, and massive concrete structures gave us vague clues to an interesting past. Yet no one seemed to know what the mine was for or what its history was. Thanks to some sleuthing, we now know its full story.

The San Gabriels above us were heavily mined for gold and other minerals. There was even a "Big Tujunga Mining District" in the late 1800s. In the Verdugo Mountains, there was mining as well. There was a silica mine and three exploited graphite deposits. One of these graphite deposits was developed into a very successful mine with a mill and processing plant.

The graphite was first discovered there in 1886. Specimens brought back to L.A. showed good amounts of "plumbago," the old term for graphite. Graphite had a wide range of industrial uses from steel production to lubricants and, of course, pencil lead. Our local graphite was suitable for paint and foundry facings.

The mine was soon opened in a little canyon of the Verdugos, and ore was brought down and freighted to L.A. The land the mine sat on began to be bought and sold in a speculative fashion, reportedly at one point fetching $100,000. The boosters of Crescenta Valley were abuzz with hopes that development of the mine would result in a railroad into the valley.

By 1899, the mine was in full swing. A large tunnel was producing graphite mixed with granite. Wooden tracks brought ore carts to a crude processing site where a gas engine operated a crusher, mixer, and dryer to separate the graphite from the granite. It was yielding several grades of graphite valued from $10 per ton to $125 per ton for the highest grade. A water tunnel above the mine supplied water for the operation.

In 1918, the land was owned by the Hostetter family, who apparently lived near the site on the Hostetter Ranch and in Los Angeles. The fire road coming off La Tuna Canyon Road today is named Hostetter Road. The mine was leased to a corporation, the Standard Graphite Company, who issued stock to finance a larger mill for processing the graphite. Initially, a huge mill was to be built in Montrose that would employ seventy-five men.

Instead, the big mill was built on the hillside about 1 mile below the mine. We can speculate that mining carts on steel rails carried the ore down from the mine to a cliff above the mill. The ore was then loaded into carts that were winched several hundred yards down on nearly vertical tracks to a stamp mill and crusher just above the larger mill. The mill was the latest in technology, a floatation mill. The crushed ore was fed through a series of water-filled tanks. The water was agitated and fed with compressed air, which caused the lighter graphite flakes to separate from the granite. The graphite floated to the top in a froth that was skimmed off. The graphite-filled froth was dried, filtered, processed further, and fed into barrels for shipment.

But in the 1920s, graphite began to be shipped in from Madagascar and other countries, where it could be produced much cheaper. Unable to compete, the mine and mill closed around 1930. It briefly reopened during the Second World War, when the war interrupted international shipping. Since that time, perhaps in the 1950s, the mine caved in, the tracks were removed, and the processing equipment scrapped, leaving only the empty shell of the mill.

At the mine site today, there are several pieces of ore cart track laying around, along with a lot of water and compressed air piping. Flat spots and rail tie footings indicate where the ore carts rolled to the cliff above the mill, where the winch remains,

This is the entrance to the graphite mill, with a man standing in the entrance to give it scale. This massive, century-old concrete structure goes back about 200 feet. On the hillside above it are the remains of the rock crusher and various other ore-processing machines. This mill is about 400 yards from the 210 Freeway, and 100 yards from a well-traveled fire road. Yet it is so covered in brush that no one knows it is there. (*Author*)

half-buried in the hillside. The mill still stands—a massive concrete structure, now completely hidden by decades of overgrowth. It is only 400 yards from the 210 Freeway, yet is invisible until one bumps into it while bushwacking through the thick brush. It is just another piece of our valley's history, waiting to be rediscovered.

Mystery "Bridges" Across the Freeway

There are what appear to be unused bridges over the 210 Freeway, three in total, in a 1-mile section between Rosemont Avenue and Angeles Crest Highway. They appear to be vehicular bridges but are not accessible to traffic. Some have speculated by their appearance that they are bridges that had been built in anticipation of future road development.

But they are actually covered flood control channels going over the freeway, like "square tubes" or flumes. They are substantial enough to appear to be street overpasses. The

What appears to be an unused bridge over the 210 Freeway is actually a viaduct, a rectangular tube, carrying the water coming down from Pickens Canyon. This one is between Rosemont and Briggs. (*Author*)

Pickens Flood Control Channel crosses the 210 between Rosemont and Briggs. There is another to the east between Briggs and Ocean View that is the Hall-Beckley Flood Control Channel, and a third one further to the east between the 2 Freeway interchange and Memorial Park, which drains Winery Canyon. That one is especially interesting because you can actually walk across it. The La Cañada Trail Council opened it for public access as a section of their Cross Town Trail. You can access it by turning off Foothill onto Indiana Avenue. The entrance to the bridge is at the intersection of Indiana and Curran Street.

Montrose's Auto Assembly Plant—The Flintridge Motor Manufacturing Corporation

It may surprise you to find out that in February 1957, the Flintridge Motor Manufacturing Corporation established an auto assembly plant in Montrose at 3724 Park Place. The building is still there and has the signature architectural look of a building of that era.

A small article in the local paper in 1957 outlined some information about the assembly plant provided by the president Harry Lindsay. The cars they were assembling were German DKWs. The parts were produced in Germany and shipped to the U.S. for assembly, with some manufacturing to be done at the assembly site. Flintridge Motors was licensed to produce the cars and slap their own name on them. They assembled a small sedan and an early RV: the Flintridge Caravan. The Flintridge Caravan resembled a sheet-metal travel trailer bolted to a small van front end.

The DKW design that these Flintridge models were built on had some features we would consider ahead of their time. The engines were mounted transversely in the vehicle, and drove the front wheels, both features that most cars today have. However, the engines were 900-cc three-cylinder two-stroke engines that produced only 38 hp. This was at a time when most American cars had big V8's, or at least six-cylinder engines producing horsepower measured in the hundreds. But apparently, the physically tiny engine was strong for its size, and with proper gearing, pushed the Flintridge cars along at a respectable speed, probably trailing a column of acrid smoke typical of two-stroke engines of that era.

Flintridge Motors had its own showroom at 442 Foothill, across the street from today's La Cañada Trader Joes, and was part of a nationwide group of DKW dealers. Their advertising played to the strengths of the odd little cars. They called the DKW "unique" and trumpeted that the cars had front-wheel drive and German craftsmanship. They told potential buyers that the odd little engine got up to 35 miles per gallon, had only seven moving parts, and could push the car along at 75 miles per hour. They said about the engine that "3 equals 6," meaning that their three-cylinder engine produced the same power as a six-cylinder one.

It was at this point in 1957 that Flintridge Motors entered into a partnership to produce a sports car that has become somewhat legendary: the Flintridge Darren. The concept of fiberglass car bodies was relatively new, and a few cutting-edge designers were working with the idea of taking production cars and "reskinning" with a fiberglass body to emulate the successful Corvette. One of the most successful designers was Howard "Dutch" Darren. He was approached by investors willing to pay to have a production fiberglass sports car designed for the DKW chassis. He was directed to the Flintridge Motor Manufacturing Corporation of Montrose, who provided him with a DKW sedan to work out his design on. He cut away the boxy DKW auto body and sculpted a clay prototype on it. From there, Flintridge Motors produced tooling for a visually stunning fiberglass body to attach to the DKW chassis.

The design was a hit with reviewers. The car was low and sleek, with raised tailfins. It slightly resembled the Carmen Ghia. The tiny motor under the featherweight body produced some impressive performance, and the beautiful convertible could seat five—unusual for a sports car. It was decided to move the Flintridge Darren production line to Santa Ana, where the fiberglass body panels were being produced. Only about twenty of these interesting sports cars were produced, before slow sales dictated an end to production.

From here, we lose track of what became of the Flintridge Motor Manufacturing Corporation. An internet search turns up a Flintridge travel trailer produced in 1959, but that is the end of the trail. Not a single legendary Flintridge Darren survives

Three Cylinders Equals Six Passengers

GERMANY provides the machinery, and California the body.

THIS IS the Darrin Mark II DKW which will go into a 10 car per week production schedule in the middle of April. The two-door, six-passenger body, styled by Dutch Darrin, will be available in either steel or Fiberglas, and is completely finished by Flintridge Motors, La Cañada, Calif. The chassis is Auto Union's DKW sedan design, built in West Germany and shipped to California for installation of the seven-piece custom body. The seven units include the front and rear sections, the hood and deck lid, the two doors, and the hard top. Part of the top, the front section, is removable in landau style, or a completely removable top is optionally available. The grille has been changed since the photo at left was taken; a plain mesh will be used instead of the rings. Price will be approximately $790 more than a stock DKW sedan, or about $2990.

40 MOTOR TREND/APRIL 1957

Here is a photo feature from *Motor Trend* magazine in 1957. It shows a prototype of the Flintridge Darren sports car. Although the text claims it would be produced in La Canada, that was a little bit of upscale marketing. It was actually slated to be produced at the Flintridge Motor Manufacturing Corporation of Montrose. (*undiscoveredclassics.com*)

today, making for an interesting but elusive chapter in the automobile history of the Crescenta Valley.

The Lost Wagon Trail of Angeles Crest

It is rare to find someone who knows the history of the aborted first incarnation of Angeles Crest Highway, cut by hand in 1873. The Soledad Road, or Capt. Moore's Road, was to be a major freight wagon route across the San Gabriels between the Mojave Desert and Los Angeles, and was to pass right through the Crescenta Cañada Valley. The project was pure speculation in a boom period of Los Angeles history, and it failed, but not before it was partially built.

In the 1860s, the Cerro Gordo Mine (located in the Inyo Mountains, east of the Owens Valley) began pumping out high-grade silver ore. Smelters reduced the ore to bullion, and thousands of silver ingots began to stack up at Cerro Gordo. In 1868, an enterprising Los Angeles Frenchman, Remi Nadeau, was contracted to haul the bullion the 200 miles to Los Angeles. The silver was stacked on a small steamship to cross the then-full Owens Lake, where it was met by Nadeau's freight operation. His eighteen-mule heavy-duty wagons would trudge across the Mojave Desert and traverse the San Gabriels through Saugus, basically following the route of the 14 Freeway, then down to Los Angeles, and on to Wilmington. This freight route was bringing about $50,000 worth of silver a day through the streets of L.A., then a town of about 5,000, and was making a fortune for everyone associated with it. Inevitably, other businessmen would try for a piece of the action.

In 1873, investors lined up a plan for a cut-off road—a shorter wagon trail through the San Gabriels to the Mojave Desert. Engineers from the defunct Mormon Battalion, who had built Fort Moore in Downtown L.A. in 1847, and then disbanded, were employed to map a route and begin construction. They cut a heavy wagon road north from L.A. and up through Verdugo Canyon.

Following the path Verdugo Road takes today, they turned east at today's Montrose and switchbacked up the hill past today's Vons to where the Verdugo Hospital is. At that point, they made a straight diagonal path across the sagebrush of La Cañada to the point where Angeles Crest Highway turns to head up the mountain. They quickly cut a road into the wilderness, basically following the route the Crest takes, but with many more twists and curves.

They got all the way up to Dark Canyon, about 5 miles up on the modern highway, before the road builders got word that the Southern Pacific Railroad would be laying

This is an aerial view from 1930 of the progress on building Angeles Crest Highway. The view shows the beginning of the curving portion of the highway above La Canada, where today it passes by the La Canada Flintridge Country Club golf course and continues up the mountain. Just above the newly cut highway, a smaller road is visible. That is the 1873 Soledad Highway, portions of which still remain. (*Historical Society of the Crescenta Valley*)

tracks on the current freight wagon route through Saugus, thus destroying the trade for freight wagons hauling silver into L.A. The Soledad Road was abandoned. The road is visible in a couple very old landscape photos of La Cañada but was never really employed as a road. The mountain portion is shown on an 1877 map of the Lanterman/Williams tracts in the Crescenta–Cañada Valley.

The last trace of the roadbed through C.V., a small section next to Verdugo Road just below the hospital, was buried by the 2/210 Interchange in the early 1970s. But some say that the old road still exists in bits and pieces in the San Gabriel Mountains above La Cañada, and indeed the author has found short sections of very old roadbed in my hikes. If they are indeed remnants of the Soledad Road is guesswork. It is hard to believe that the road bed could survive this long. The most visible section is just past the last houses on the way up. Look up to your left as you pass the wide construction turnout, and you will clearly see traces of a very old road on the hillsides above the highway.

Next time you drive the Crest; imagine what could have been—burley, cursing teamsters driving eighteen-mule teams in front of wagons carrying tons of silver, pulling hard on the brakes, the rear wheels chained and skidding as they dropped down into La Cañada.

Rebal's Mad House

The "madman" method of retail sales was a California phenomenon, starting in the early 1940s with Madman Muntz, a used car dealer in Glendale who rejected traditional salesman concepts. He instead adopted the persona of an insane person ("I must be crazy to sell at these prices!") who would generate publicity via crazy stunts. Madman Muntz would threaten to smash his cars with a sledgehammer if they did not sell that day and proclaimed, "I buy 'em retail and sell 'em wholesale—It's more fun that way!" The advertising scheme worked, and soon other retailers joined the "madman" sales method. California retailers like Crazy Gideon and Cal Worthington (and his dog Spot) have made their marks over the years, and the advertising tactic carries on today ("... or your mattress is FREEEEEE!" and "You're killing me, Larry!").

In 1947, Fred Rebal opened a market at 2931 Honolulu Avenue in Verdugo City and employed his own brand of "madman" sales. The huge sign above the store proclaimed "Rebal's Mad House—It's fun to shop at Rebal's—Have you had your fun today?" Fred Rebal was a sloganeer and shouted that at Rebal's, "a fast nickel beats a slow dime." Its location was billed as "In the heart of La Cañada-Flintridge-Alta Canyada-La Crescenta-Highway Highlands-Verdugo City-Sparr Heights-Montecito Park-Verdugo Woodlands Valley—now come up for air!" He joked about the obscurity of Verdugo City, billing his new market as the "store that made Verdugo City famous." The store's hours were displayed as "visiting hours."

Not surprisingly, Rebal's newspaper ads were hilarious. In a gift promotion for Mother's Day, Father's Day, and graduation, the early summer ad featured a picture of Santa with the admonition "Don't wait until Christmas" and "Santa Says: It's more fun to give that to receive—But it's enormously satisfying to receive!" Rebal's reminded readers that "this is National Verdugo City Gift Week" and that they offered "free gift wrapping by amateurs."

Rebal's also promoted an engaging atmosphere for his store with such slogans as "Your friendly family store with that personal touch to make your visits more fun!" and "We're big enough to serve you with the largest selection ... Small enough to know you." Fred Rebal imparted a personal feel to his store by featuring his name and photo in his advertising. He held promotions that encouraged the community to come out. His one-year anniversary featured free pony rides for the kids, a Halloween costume contest, and a special show put on by movie-star and honorary mayor of Montrose, Dennis Morgan. In the early 1950s, he showed free outdoor movies projected on the side of the building. It was a big deal when the dwarf Billy Barty made an appearance.

But it was getting tough for the small "markets" to compete with the growing "supermarkets." By the early 1960s, it appears the Rebal family sold the store to Country Cousins, another market, although Fred seems to have still maintained a presence in Verdugo City with the ownership of a nearby liquor store. With this new retail alcohol trade, he apparently could still ask his customers, "Have you had your fun today?"

Country Cousins soon became Phil's Market. Sometime in the 1990s, Phil's became Sparky's Apple Mart, and Sparky's became Cordon's Ranch Market. Cordon's was once again a "fun" store to shop in as they filled the niche of an ethnic food market. Shelves were stocked with foods from Mexico, South America, Armenia, Russia, and European nations. Cordon's recently closed, and the rumor went around that the old building was finished—to be torn down for condos.

However, it was not. It continued as an ethnic foods market for a couple years under another name. Recently, it was completely remodeled in a modern style and broken up into a variety of smaller spaces, all of which at the time of this writing are up for lease.

Tujunga's Hollywood Bowl

Natural amphitheaters in canyons have long been a place for people to gather and listen to musical performances. The sloping of the hillsides gives everyone a good view, and the addition of a band shell helps to project the sound out to the audience. Amphitheaters and band shells are popular across the world, and most big cities have one. Due to their shape, they are often nicknamed "bowls." Of course, the most famous is the Hollywood Bowl. It was built in 1922 as a community space and a performance spot for local orchestras, but because of its location near Hollywood, it soon became a world-class venue. The closest bowl to us is the Starlight Bowl, built into a canyon in 1950 on the other side of the Verdugo Mountains overlooking Burbank.

In the late 1940s, a massive amphitheater, nearly the size of the Hollywood Bowl, was planned for Tujunga. It was proposed to seat 15,000. For comparison, the modern Hollywood Bowl seats 17,500. A local outdoor amphitheater had long been a dream for poet and playwright John Steven McGroarty, who built his home in Tujunga, and in the 1940s, that dream was taken up by the Sunland–Tujunga Bowl Association.

In early 1948, the dream was kicked into high gear when an anonymous donor offered a large piece of land at the north end of McVine Avenue, less than 1 mile from Foothill Boulevard. The donated land had the natural "bowl" required, and there was ample parking on empty land below the proposed amphitheater. Sound engineers proclaimed the site acoustically perfect. A rendering showed the amphitheater wrapped nicely in a fold of the mountains, the audience facing southwest, with a bandshell at the bottom. Just behind the audience was a ridgeline, and below that, Big Tujunga Canyon. It was a visually spectacular location. Even before the bowl was built, 3,000 people showed up for an Easter sunrise service on the site.

While the Bowl Association began to work on building a venue, the community got to work on creating performing groups. A Sunland–Tujunga Symphony Orchestra was formed and performed at Sunland Park and school auditoriums. An operatic group was formed with their first performance to be the opera, *Carmen*. As the bowl was not built yet, *Carmen* was performed at Pinewood Elementary's auditorium to several sold-out audiences.

Perhaps the most remarkable performing group formed was the Sunland–Tujunga Chorus. It was headed by the famous Italian composer Rico Marcelli. Although Marcelli

This crude concept drawing of the proposed 15,000-seat Sunland-Tujunga Bowl was distributed in 1948 to drum-up enthusiasm for the project. (*Little Landers Historical Society*)

began as a composer of operas, he found his greatest fame as an orchestral conductor. He was the conductor (and composer) for many of the great silent movie houses, most famously for arranging and conducting the music for *Salome*. He later transitioned to conducting orchestras backing radio shows like Fibber McGee and Molly. He retired to Sunland. The Sunland–Tujunga Chorus debuted on KHJ radio.

But obviously, the bowl never happened. In the fall of 1948, everything suddenly fell apart. The site in a residential neighborhood was not zoned for a big venue like this, so the city of L.A. initially nixed the concept. Petitions were circulated in the community and hundreds signed. A hearing was set for August to work through the zoning issues. A variance was granted, but with very stringent restrictions. The seating capacity was drastically reduced to 4,000. Fire restrictions, increased water supply, and paved roads leading to the bowl were all made requirements, ballooning the cost of the bowl.

The bowl association grudgingly accepted the conditions, but a few days later the killing blow was struck. During escrow, the anonymous donor, suddenly and without warning, withdrew his donation offer. This, combined with the zoning restrictions, was the end for the Sunland–Tujunga Bowl Association. The president of the group resigned, and the association disbanded. Apparently, all the performing groups that had formed faded away.

The bowl site was graded and developed. It is fun to think about this major concert venue that would have rivaled the Hollywood Bowl. It probably would have changed the fabric of Sunland–Tujunga and made it a magnet for the arts, but it was a momentary flash of a dream that faded quickly.

A Railroad to the Top of the Verdugos

In 1912, a plan was drawn up to bring people to the summit via a "funicular railway" similar to the Mt. Lowe Railway in Altadena, at that time a major tourist attraction, but first I should explain what a funicular railway is.

Funicular (from the Latin *funis*, or "rope") generally describes railroads specifically designed to carry passengers or freight up a steep incline via a weighted cable. This system has been in use for hundreds of years all over the world, and in booming early twentieth-century Los Angeles, there were several in operation. Notable were Angels Flight and Court Flight in Downtown L.A., the Mount Washington Railway just north of downtown, two in Avalon on Catalina Island, and the granddaddy of them all—the Mount Lowe Railway above Altadena. Mt. Lowe, opened in 1893, was the modern-day equivalent of Disneyland to tourists and was a must-see for California vacationers. The funicular portion of the route, the "Great Incline," gave riders a spectacular 2,000-foot elevation gain. Riders can today ride a modern funicular at Magic Mountain, or better yet, the restored 110-year-old Angels Flight on Hill Street in downtown Los Angeles.

With funiculars popular in old L.A., it seems only natural that one should be planned for Glendale, then a fast-growing city. In 1912, an entrepreneur with the flamboyant name of Colonel Lewis Ginger proposed a funicular railway to be called the Glendale and Mount Verdugo Railway. Glendale's Casa Verdugo Restaurant was a wildly popular tourist destination of that era, playing off the romantic California Mission theme that was attracting thousands of visitors to Southern California from the east coast. The Mexican restaurant was located at the end of the Pacific Electric trolley line that ran up Brand Boulevard, and Col. Ginger had a vision of construction a connecting railway from the restaurant to the top of Mt. Thom. Ginger initially proposed that the big trolley cars would drive straight onto a platform on the funicular's tracks and would remain level as they lifted up the incline to the summit, with the passengers never having to leave their seats. Pacific Electric owner Henry Huntington was not thrilled with this scheme, and Ginger then planned for angled and stepped cars similar to the Mt. Lowe incline or Angles Flight. The route was to have four or five stations along the way and a big visitor's center at the summit.

Imagine the spectacular views from the top. Unlike the view from Mt. Lowe which was only toward the sea, the view from Mt. Thom would have that sea view plus vistas to the north and west, across the undeveloped Crescenta–Cañada Valley, and deep into the ranges of the San Gabriel Mountains—what a great day trip it would have been. One could take the trolley up from Los Angeles, have lunch at the Casa Verdugo, and then board the Glendale and Mt. Verdugo Railway to ascend to the top of the Verdugos for a drink and some amazing 360-degree views.

After a few months of attempting to wrangle a deal with the difficult Henry Huntington, Col. Ginger shifted his funicular plans east to the Verdugo Canyon. Verdugo Park was then a popular picnic spot, and a rail line brought hundreds each weekend to the stream-fed verdant "wilds" of Verdugo Canyon. This funicular would have run again to Mt. Thom, this time from the northern end of Verdugo Park, basically following the route Sunshine Drive takes today.

But after over a year of financial wrangling, Colonel Lewis Ginger's scheme to make the Verdugo Mountains a tourist attraction was running out of steam, and the plans were abandoned. The Verdugos were to remain the urban wilderness they still are today.

The Saga of Tujunga's Weatherwolde Castle

Both Crescenta/Cañada Valley and neighboring Sunland/Tujunga have long traditions of castle-building. There were several built here in our early years, about half of which still survive, notably La Cañada's "Pink Castle" and Tujunga's Blarney Castle, but the most compelling story comes from Tujunga's Weatherwolde Castle on Commerce Avenue, which was saved from the bulldozer by the community's outrage in 2005.

The castle's origin has two stories—the legend and the fact. The legend is this: Marcel Dumas, a homesick French ex-patriot, was married to an exiled countess. He wanted to install his blue-blooded wife in a chateau worthy of her noble roots. He had a Norman-style castle built for her in Tujunga and named it Weatherwolde. Several years later, he lost it in a dramatic high-stakes poker game. The reality was that Dumas and his wife (not a countess) were indeed born in locations with exotic French names—New

Orleans and St. Louis respectively—and had the stylish castle built in Tujunga in 1928. Dumas lost the castle, not in a high-stakes poker game, but because he stopped paying taxes on the property after the crash of 1929.

By the late 1930s, the Harris family were able to pick up the property for a paltry $7,000 in back taxes. It is at this point that reality lived up to the legend, for Mrs. Harris was the secretary to Hollywood legend David O. Selznik, producer of *Gone with the Wind*. The castle's exotic appearance and the amazing landscaping the Harris family installed made the castle a magnet for celebrities of that era, and Bela Lugosi, Orson Welles, and Robert Mitchum were guests at parties held there. The Harris family lovingly maintained and accented the castle until 1974, when it was bought by an antique dealer Yvonne Kenward.

Kenward only had the castle for five years until 1979, but it is from her imagination that the castle's legend, and its name—"Weatherwolde"—sprung. The name was made-up supposedly an ancient Anglo-Saxon word for a place of shelter, but it stuck, mainly due to Kenward's promotion of the castle and her associated antique business.

In 1979, a husband/wife duo in the entertainment industry purchased it as their third house, and it was in those twenty-five years that the house became so overgrown and hidden from view that the neighbors literally forgot it was there. In 2005, it was bought by a local developer who intended to demolish it and build new homes. On a Friday, his crew cut away all the overgrowth and broke up the extensive patios and rockwork, leaving the castle to finish off on Monday.

The neighbors were flabbergasted to find a full-on castle magically sitting on a bare lot, where a thick forest had once stood. Some in the community reacted by entering the castle and stripping it of anything of value—from stained-glass windows to plumbing fixtures to a wrought-iron spiral staircase. Others rallied to save the castle, frantically pulling together various local preservation groups and contacting news agencies. On

This is what was revealed in 2005 when workers cleared the foliage from Weatherwolde Castle, prior to its scheduled demolition. It had been so overgrown for so long that neighbors did not even know it was there. The community banded together to save the castle, and today it is fully restored. (*Bill Weisman*)

Monday morning, the sun rose to a mob of protesters in front of the house, along with several news trucks and two news helicopters. The demolition crew pulled up in their truck, took one look at the crowd, and just kept on driving. The city of L.A. rallied to the cause as well, and a stop-work order was issued. Despite the objections of the developer, the castle was declared a city historical landmark.

William Malouf, a local musician and home restorer, heard about the tussle and drove by to investigate. It was love at first sight, and after lengthy negotiations, he purchased the stripped castle from the developer. What happened next was like a scene in a cheesy movie. The stolen items from the castle began to reappear, until almost everything that had been stolen was back at Weatherwolde. Nine years later, Malouf and his family completed the restoration. It is another piece of our heritage saved from destruction—a fairy-tale ending to a fairy-tale castle.

5
Weird Events

Duck and Cover: The 1955 A-Bomb Drill

For a scant four years after WWII, the U.S. was the only nation with "the bomb." That all changed in 1949 when the Soviet Union detonated their first nuclear device. The U.S. was shocked that the USSR had caught up with us so quickly, and we raced ahead with our arms programs. That was the beginning of the "Cold War"—a chilling time in history in which the only thing preventing one side from attacking the other was that in any exchange of fire, both sides would be completely destroyed.

In 1955, the saber-rattling was getting particularly loud. At Bikini Atoll, above ground testing was producing blasts a thousand times more powerful than the Hiroshima blast. Very real plans began to be put into place to deal with the reality of a nuclear attack. A nationwide drill called "Operation Alert" was planned for June 15, 1955, in which fifty-five U.S. cities, including Los Angeles, would drill as though they had been hit by "relatively small" bombs, in the 1–5-megaton range. What is "relatively small" when talking about nuclear bombs? The 15-megaton bomb dropped on Bikini Atoll in 1954 would have killed every person in an area the size of New Jersey, and a 100-megaton bomb was developed by the USSR in 1961. So, relatively speaking, they were relatively small.

In this drill, some cities would have advance warning, a steady wail from the air raid sirens. That meant that an attack was coming, and everyone should get to a shelter or prepare to evacuate. Other cities would get no pre-warning, just that they were under attack right now, notified by an undulating wail from the sirens. That meant duck and cover.

Here in Los Angeles, the test was to come at midday on Wednesday June 15. At 9 a.m., the alert would come that bombers were incoming (this was before intercontinental missiles). At 11:46 a.m., the warning would come to send people to shelters, and at 12:45, three pretend bombs would hit metro Los Angeles. The first would hit south of Downtown L.A. at Florence and Broadway, followed by two more. The closest to us would hit Hollywood, at the intersection of Santa Monica and Gower. Projections were that lethal amounts of radiation would kill everyone in Glendale, up to the Verdugo Woodlands area. Those trying to flee to the relative safety of the Crescenta Valley would bottleneck by Glendale College, and few would make it through. Glendale would be considered untenable, the entire area contaminated. Glendale's four hospitals would be too radiated to treat the thousands of injured. Transportation would be paralyzed; all utilities would no longer exist.

The drill was to last about twenty-four hours and would for the most part test the resources of emergency personnel. How real the drill would be seems to have been on a city-by-city basis. It appears from newspaper reports that here in C.V., the sirens were not even sounded. But in other cities they were, and citizens were to act as though the attack were real. In Los Angeles, government workers went to shelters when the sirens sounded, while most people were just confused. In Denver and Houston, the emergency personnel actually evacuated large numbers out of the city. In New York, 17,000 spectators in Yankee Stadium simply ignored the sirens and sat in place waiting for the game to start.

The drill was deemed moderately successful, but the projected death toll from that first strike was sobering. Nationwide, 5 million were "killed," 5 million "injured," and 10 million made homeless refugees. In L.A., the death toll was 800,000, with over 1 million heading north and south as homeless refugees. Here in the Crescenta Valley, we would be relatively safe until wind spread the radiation to us. We could not even enter the Glendale area.

We think of the 1950s and '60s as "happy days," but there was a darkness then, and a lot of fear. It was not "if" but "when." A UCLA scientist declared at a wrap-up session after the drill that the best way to calm a frightened nation is to present the facts of what would happen in a real attack. He then presented the fact that we could write off as dead anyone living in a large city. Sadly, his facts did little to calm a frightened nation.

In 1969 The Black Panthers Came to Glendale

The year 1969 was tumultuous, particularly on college campuses. Even tiny Glendale Community College was subject to controversy. Early that year, the student-led Human Relations Council had submitted a list of proposed on-campus speakers for the next year. Included in the list was a representative from the Black Panther Party. That was immediately denied by GCC officials.

Needless to say, the students fought the denial. There was much back and forth on the issue in early 1969, with some incendiary public meetings. Ultimately, the matter went to court, and with the backing of the ACLU, the students prevailed on a free-speech basis. The Black Panthers were to speak at GCC.

The contrasts and ironies of "past versus the present" are noteworthy. Here are some examples. Recently, conservative activists protested the denial of some far-right speakers to speak on college campuses. In the 1960s, the opposite was the case. Recently, right-wing activists have openly carried firearms in some high-profile demonstrations, including armed protesters entering the Michigan State Capitol. In 1960s California, the exact same thing happened, but on the opposite end of the political spectrum.

A quick historical "lesson in irony" to show how much has and has not changed: In the 1960s, it was legal to openly carry a loaded gun in California. The Black Panthers took advantage of that by carrying firearms. They formed "police patrols" in which they would follow police cars. If a black driver was pulled over, the Black Panthers would quietly stand nearby displaying loaded weapons—perfectly legal, but intimidating nonetheless. There was a strong backlash in Sacramento, and Republican Don Mulford introduced a bill in 1967 that prohibited openly carrying loaded firearms. Black Panthers, carrying loaded rifles and handguns (still legal as the bill had not yet been enacted), entered the capitol building to protest the bill. They were disarmed, and escorted out. Yet as a result, the bill outlawing what today would be called "open carry" passed (ironically with the strong backing of the NRA) and has been the law ever since. Gov. Reagan commented that there was "no reason why on the street today a citizen should be carrying loaded weapons."

In October 1969, the now disarmed Black Panthers were invited to speak in the GCC auditorium. They chose as their spokesperson Elaine Brown, a relatively new member of the Panthers. About 800 GCC students attended. Elaine Brown opened with a bang. "All power to the people! Death to pigs!" She greeted Glendale as the home to "Birchers" and the American Nazi Party.

> Our [Panthers] purpose is not to run through Glendale and Orange County and kill all the little white babies. Our purpose is to create a human arena that will bring about changes in this system. Our purpose is to create a climate where we can all be humans.

She further advocated for a redistribution of wealth. She predicted authoritarian changes to the Constitution that would bring about further oppression, but she advocated strong resistance. "The power belongs to the people. The streets belong to the people. It's up to the people to take them!" She chastised "little pig Nixon and lesser pig Reagan."

The audience was politely quiet through the forty-five-minute talk, but she lost many of them when she called the recent moon landing a hoax filmed on a Hollywood stage. About 200 students left at that point.

She ended the speech by quoting Eldridge Cleaver: "We shall have our manhood. We shall have it or the world will be leveled in our attempt to gain it. All power to the people!"

What became of the fiery Elaine Brown? She was instrumental in many of the Panthers' social welfare programs, and rose to the position of Chairman of the Panthers from 1974 to 1977. She resigned due to misogyny in the leadership. Today, she is an author and activist for prison reform. But in 1969 Glendale, she was the cutting edge of the black power movement.

The California Wine Industry Started in … Glendale?

That is a provocative title, but it may very well be true. There is evidence to suggest that the first secular (meaning outside of the missions) wine production in California was done by none other than our own Jose Maria Verdugo at his rancho in what is now North Glendale.

The origin of this interesting theory comes from local historian Stuart Byles in his fascinating book *Los Angeles Wine*. Byles traces the history of wine production in the

Los Angeles area, starting with the wine-making operations of San Gabriel Mission in the late 1700s, to the growth of the Los Angeles wine industry inspired by French immigrants in the 1800s. The wines of Los Angeles were significant to U.S. wine sales in the 1800s. In that time period, the term "California wine" actually meant wine from Los Angeles. It was not until almost the turn of the twentieth century that the L.A. vineyards began to be replaced by housing subdivisions and the California wine industry moved north to Napa-Sonoma.

As Byles researched his book, he came across a quote from the seminal book on the history of the American wine industry, Thomas Pinney's *History of Wine in America.* The quote read: "Jose Maria Verdugo may have planted the first private (non-Mission) vineyard in California on his Rancho San Rafael." That is a heady theory, that the first secular and possibly first commercial wine-making operation in California was on Verdugo's rancho here in Glendale. This sent Byles on a search for more evidence of this.

The Roman Catholic Missions that were established in California depended on wine for their religious rites, along with daily consumption. Initially, wine had to be brought up from Mexico, and it was expensive and in short supply. According to historians, the first grape cuttings arrived in California in 1778 and made their way up the chain of missions. "Mission grapes" were probably a mixture of a Spanish variety and some of the native grapes of North and South America. Eventually, San Gabriel Mission became the most prolific of all the wine-producing missions. In 1784, a corporal of the guard at San Gabriel Mission, Jose Maria Verdugo, applied for a land grant in what is now Glendale and Burbank.

That he took grape cuttings from the Mission to his new rancho is without doubt. Wine was an important part of meals for the early Californios, and they had to make their own. Verdugo established extensive crops on his property, along with irrigation systems fed by the Los Angeles River and Verdugo Creek. Jose Verdugo actually referred to his rancho by a nickname, "La Zanja," Spanish for "the water ditch", which attests to a robust irrigation system. There are a few references to his large orchards and fields, and in his will, Verdugo designates an heir for his vineyards.

So, Verdugo had vineyards, but where were they? Probably near his house, as proximity of the vines for tending and winemaking would be advantageous. But where was his house? No one knows for sure. It probably would not have been near the L.A. River, which had a tendency to flood and spread out. That would put it nearer to the Verdugo Mountains, in North Glendale. The memory of someone who came to the area in 1865 put "the oldest Verdugo house" in North Glendale around where the intersection of Kenneth Road and Pacific is today. That may have been his home, along with an "old orchard" noted on maps in the Rossmoyne area. The Verdugo Adobe we all know in Verdugo Canyon was his daughter's house, not his, but he left that land to her in his will, along with his vineyards. Is that where his original vineyards were? Were they in the Verdugo Canyon, irrigated with water coming down from the Crescenta Valley?

Granted, this is all circumstantial evidence, and Byles does not make any conclusions, but it is a likely scenario. It is doubtful that Glendale will be putting "The Birthplace of California Wine" on their "Welcome to Glendale" signs. We cannot prove it. It is just a fun theory to mull over while sipping some California wine.

Gun Crazy—A Movie Filmed in Montrose in 1950

One of the most famous scenes in cinematography, a filmed robbery of a Montrose bank, comes from an obscure "film-noir" piece released in 1950. It is a three-and-a-half-minute-long "single take" inside a moving car—a significant feat in those days. What makes it even more remarkable is that it was guerilla-style filmmaking—the busy midday street, Honolulu Avenue, was unregulated, much of the dialogue was ad-libbed, and save for the actors, none of the shoppers and other cars were aware that a movie was being shot.

The plot of *Gun Crazy* has much of what made 1967's *Bonnie and Clyde* such a big hit—a murderous romance with a sexual tension that fairly crackles, lots of action, and a peek into the criminal mind. Even the plot is similar—boy meets girl, boy and girl go on a violent crime spree, boy and girl die. *Gun Crazy* is well-known in film noir movie circles, and the Montrose bank robbery scene is iconic.

In that scene, we are viewing the drama from the back seat of a big 1940s sedan. We see the backs of the driver, Annie, played by diminutive Peggy Cummings, and her accomplice Bart in the passenger seat, played by John Dall. They are still in cowboy garb from their stint as carny sharpshooter performers. Through the windshield of the car, we see that we are traveling northbound on Verdugo Road approaching Montrose. We can see the much smaller trees in the center median, as they turn left onto Broadview. As the two share a cigarette and small talk, they turn right on Market Street and pass by the back of Anawalt Lumber, along with the backs of the store buildings we are so familiar

In the 1950 movie *Gun Crazy*, a pivotal scene was filmed in Montrose. Here we see bank robber Annie, behind the wheel of her getaway car. She is parked in front of the fictional Hampton Savings and Loan, actually Security First National Bank (today, the recently closed Faye's Intimate Apparel) at the corner of Honolulu and Ocean View looking west. (*YouTube*)

with. The tension builds as they wait to turn left onto Honolulu. It is obviously very crowded, a midday street with cars and shoppers. Through the front windshield, we can see Cozette's, a popular Montrose children's clothing store as they turn onto Honolulu and head toward Ocean View.

Just before the intersection, Annie pulls the car to the curb in front of a bank (which is today the recently closed Faye's) on the northeast corner of Honolulu and Ocean View. Bart exits the car to rob the bank, while Annie tensely waits behind the wheel. Bad luck as a policeman strolls around the corner. As Annie gets out of the car, the camera swings around to view through the passenger window. Annie flirts with the policeman, until Bart runs out of the bank. Annie knocks out the policeman with her gun, and she and Bart pile back in the car and drive off. They turn down Ocean View, and again on Broadview, tires squealing, then down Verdugo. The whole time, we get a perfect view of 1950 Montrose. It is an amazing time capsule.

This ground-breaking one-shot take was engineered by removing much of the back of a stretch Cadillac. The camera was loosely mounted in the rear-seat area, with the operator riding on a jockey saddle atop a greased board. Mics were hidden in the car, and two soundmen rode on the roof of the car with a boom mic to catch the exterior dialog. The only people in the camera's view aware this was a movie were the actors playing the two bank robbers and the policeman. It had never been done before.

The movie was written by the famous screenwriter Dalton Trumbo. This was during Trumbo's McCarthy-era fight with the House Un-American Activities Committee. The blacklisted writer used a pseudonym for the film, but the screenplay is riveting.

The movie flopped at the box office but is today recognized as a true gem of filmmaking. The Montrose bank robbery scene is a triumph of cinematography that is still talked about today. For us here in C.V., it is a historical gem. The scene is easily found on YouTube; it is an amazing ride.

High Speed Rail, Las Vegas to La Cañada? The Crystal Lake Freeway?

It is fun to write about things that could have been here in the valley, but that never panned out. In the past, this author has written about plans to turn the valley into a reservoir, construct a racetrack at C.V. Park, build Montrose Junior High, and the wholesale development of the Verdugo Mountains. This time, I will write about plans to build high-speed rail and freeway over or through the San Gabriel Mountains back in 1969.

Some of you will remember the Concorde supersonic transport (SST) of the 1960s, an airliner that would travel at twice the speed of sound, meaning you could go from New York to London in three hours. It was to revolutionize air transport but had some problems: it had a reputation for being incredibly loud (including sonic booms) and extremely polluting. Both those factors denied it landings and takeoffs from LAX. Instead, Palmdale was to be the L.A. hub for SST flights. L.A. purchased thousands of acres of desert for the massive Palmdale Intercontinental Airport. The airport proposal set off a land boom in Palmdale. It also changed transportation goals for L.A. to a priority of getting people back and forth from the L.A. basin to Palmdale quickly.

One proposal was construction of a high-speed rail from Las Vegas to Palmdale Intercontinental Airport, which would continue into a tunnel piercing the San Gabriel Mountains. After 14 miles under the mountains, the train would exit at La Cañada, then continue to L.A. This 300-mph train would take international SST passengers landing in Palmdale either to Las Vegas in an hour or to L.A. in minutes. This proposal had the advantage of money buy-in from Las Vegas.

Other proposals were either a vehicular tunnel or two cross-mountain freeways. The tunnel concept would again be 14 miles in length, again exiting in La Cañada. That would have made it the longest vehicular tunnel in the world, eclipsing the then longest tunnel in Switzerland (7.2 miles) twice over. Since then, a longer tunnel of 15.2 miles has been built in Norway.

The cross-mountain freeway concept had two proposed freeways. The first was to extend the 2 Freeway over the San Gabriels. In 1969, the 2 Freeway was already planned to end at Foothill and Hilliard, as it does today. This new concept would continue the freeway up through Alta Canyada, and across the mountains until it connected with the 14 Freeway, which was already under construction. This was to be called the 2/249 Freeway. The 2/249 Freeway would flow an estimated 96,000 vehicles a day through La Cañada by 1980. For comparison, approximately 160,000 to 180,000 vehicles a day flow through C.V. on the 210 Freeway.

The other proposal for a cross-mountain freeway was to be a second freeway in addition to the 2/249. This freeway would rise from the San Gabriel Valley about where the 605 connects with the 210, cross the mountains, and enter the Palmdale area at Valyermo. This was to be called the Crystal Lake Freeway.

Any of these concepts would have been massive engineering undertakings, but at that time they were considered vital, even urgent. The SST was the wave of the future, and other aerospace companies were working on SST concepts that would carry nearly as many passengers as the 747. This Palmdale-based airport was going to happen, and transportation to and from it would be vital.

But as we know, the SST concept never really took off (pun intended), due largely to public perception of its cost and environmental issues, and the Palmdale "Intercontinental" Airport was never built. Interesting today to think that the high-speed rail tunnel and the various cross-mountain freeway concepts were considered a done deal over fifty years ago.

When Indy Cars Roared in Montrose

A little-known aspect of the history of the Indianapolis 500 is the central role that Glendale, and by extension the Crescenta Valley, played in Indy car development and history. Glendale was a powerhouse of race car production from the 1920s into the '60s, building powerful innovative engines and car bodies that dominated the racing scene. The Crescenta Valley also played a part in this racing renaissance. The famous

Winfield Brothers hailed from La Cañada, along with several other less famous drivers and inventors.

Montrose played a role as well, particularly in the 1920s and '30s, as it was home to the machine shop of racecar builder Paul Fromm. Fromm was one of the early American developers of the famed "Hisso" racing engine. The Hisso had been adapted from the Spanish Hispano-Suiza aircraft engine, a powerful V-8 mass-produced in WWI, and acquired cheaply by car racers after the war. One bank of the vee was cut off, and the resulting 359 cubic inch four-cylinder engine was stuffed into a racecar body. Fromm was adept at this conversion as he had a background in aeronautical engines. The resulting engine was so powerful it was banned at some racetracks.

Fromm's shop, alternately known as Valley Machine Shop and Taylor & Fromm Machine Shop, was located at 3512 Ocean View. The building is still there today and is now home to Augustine & Bailey Glass and Mirror. It is a small, nondescript building with a standard retail front to Ocean View and a large shop area facing an alley behind. But through those front doors strode some of the greats of Indy Car development—Ed Winfield, Harry Miller, and Fred Offenhauser. In the alley in the back, some of the greatest drivers fired up their newly-built race cars for the first time, legendary drivers such as Wilber Shaw and Rex Mays.

In 1933, racecar builder Paul Fromm tinkers with an engine in front of his Valley Machine Shop in Montrose. The car is the Fromm-Hisso that famous driver Rex Mays drove to Ascot championships that year. The engine was adapted from an aircraft engine, and with its straight-pipe exhaust, it must have been incredibly loud. Imagine living nearby when they were tuning their racecars. Augustine & Bailey Glass and Mirror are in the former Valley Machine Shop at 3512 Ocean View. (*Historical Society of the Crescenta Valley*)

We know about this little-known history thanks to Paul Brown, who grew up in Montrose in the 1930s. Paul wrote several memoir pieces that were published in the monthly newsletter of the Historical Society of the Crescenta Valley. As a young boy, Paul was fascinated with machines, enthralled by the robust racing scene that existed in Southern California, and even raced his home-made "soap box coasters" in the soap box derby held on the hilly portion of Slauson Boulevard in Los Angeles. He later parlayed his enthusiasm for racing into summer jobs at Paul Fromm's machine shop. Rather than paraphrase Brown's memories, I will quote what he wrote:

> Starting sometime when I was about ten-years-old, I discovered Valley Machine Shop, just below Montrose on Ocean View Boulevard. When I found that race cars were being built at Valley Machine, that building became a Mecca for me. I would stand at the door and ogle any car, under any stage of construction, and bask in my nearness to a car pictured in the newspaper, magazine or in a movie news short. I was living in the reflection of shining glory. There were people that worked in the movies and lived in Montrose who we saw from time to time, or in a Republic western film at Monte Friend's theater [Montrose Theater], but that was nothing compared to being close to a bright-colored shiny racecar that was pictured in Popular Mechanics or the Los Angeles Times. The Valley Machine Shop built cars that raced in the Indianapolis 500, the many dirt tracks, and even at Ascot Speedway in Los Angeles. Being there, within touching distance was like being close to Clark Gable or Dizzy Dean.
>
> As I became more familiar around the Valley Machine Shop, I got to know the mechanics who built the cars and the machinists who worked making parts for the cars, and for companies like Lockheed. One of the mechanics became a friend to me. His name was Johnnie Famulero, known in the shop and among racing men as "Jonnyfam." He would let me sit in a car and play make-believe behind the steering wheel. He also let me help push a racecar down Ocean View in order to start the engine. Then, the driver would steer the car down Ocean View, turn back up Verdugo, and drive to the back door of the Valley Machine Shop for work in the rear of the shop.
>
> I became a regular at the shop during the summer and when I was not busy doing some other type of work. The doors at Valley Machine Shop were always open to me. I got to know the owner, Paul Fromm, and I saw many who were involved in racing and the manufacture of speed equipment for all cars. The Winfield brothers, Ed and Bud, were regulars. They were well known for their auto engine heads, manifolds and carburetors. I had seen them bring into "Valley" a pattern and core for a new carburetor idea, ram up the mold, heat aluminum in a crucible and pour the casting, then go to the machine shop and create the carburetor. I saw the men who created the bodies for the Indianapolis cars at Curtiscraft Company in Glendale, and I saw Mr. Offenhauser, known for his high-speed engine called the "Offie." As one who hung around, I was asked from time-to-time if I would clean up the shop or to clean a machine. They always paid me something, but I would have done the cleaning free just to be there with the cars and mechanics. One time I saw famous driver Wilber Shaw at Valley Machine simply testing the seat of the car he would drive and win the 500 at Indianapolis.

> During the several years that I frequented the Valley Machine Shop I saw many cars that were being prepared for racing and some that had been brought back for repair after a race. The first cars that I remember were the cars that had an abnormally high engine compartment that housed an engine made from an Italian aircraft engine known as a Hispano-Suiza. That large engine was cut in half and adapted to racecar dimensions. The class of cars made with those engines were known as the "Hissos," and they were the ones that had the high fish-tail section that tapered into a fine vertical point at the rear of the body. The next cars I remember included the "Offies," the engine made by Offenhauser. Those engines were not as tall as earlier "Hisso" engines and permitted a much lower engine compartment with a trim, low body design.
>
> The period from my 10th birthday until I was 14 was an exciting time. I would drop in when cars were being worked on, talk to mechanics and sometimes drivers. I listened to races when Paul Fromm had a car in the race driven by somebody I had met. On one occasion I listened to a dirt track race where a driver named Kenny Pew was killed. He was one of the drivers who came by "Valley" to talk to the mechanics and test the car for comfort. Kenny's accident was a sad event and I felt the loss.

Paul Brown's memories bring to life the racing history that was made right here in the Crescenta Valley, when racecars roared up and down Ocean View Boulevard.

Richard Nixon Comes to Montrose

In October 1962, the future president held a campaign rally in Montrose, giving a speech before 2,000 enthusiastic locals. He was running for California governor on the Republican ticket, against the Democrat incumbent Governor Brown. Governor Edmund "Pat" Brown was the father of our recent Governor Jerry Brown. Nixon had been vice president to Eisenhower through the 1950s and had run unsuccessfully for president in 1960 against John F. Kennedy.

Nixon was on a campaign tour of the Los Angeles area on Saturday, October 20, 1962, and his first stop was to be Montrose at 10:30. Montrose was a friendly venue for the conservative politician. The Crescenta Valley back then leaned very far to the right, and the local newspaper, *The Ledger*, was conservative to the extreme.

On schedule that sunny Saturday morning, Nixon's motorcade drove down Honolulu escorted by carloads of pretty local girls who called themselves the "Nixonettes"—these were very different times. Also in the motorcade were several other Republican politicians. The motorcade turned south on Ocean View and into the car lot of Ed Priester Chevrolet. In a staged area strung with red, white, and blue bunting, the pretty Nixonettes shook pom-poms, while Republican State Assemblyman Frank Lanterman of La Cañada entertained the crowd by playing tunes on a portable organ.

Before Nixon took the stage, he was warmly introduced by U.S. Congressman H. Allen Smith, who was one of the more conservative members of Congress, representing California's 43rd district for almost two decades. His voting record is most notable for his strong opposition to the Civil Rights Act and the Voting Rights Act. In perhaps the ultimate irony, the 43rd district is now represented by Democrat Maxine Waters, an African-American woman.

Nixon took the stage in front of the cheering crowd and laid out his platform for governor. He led with a call for lower taxes. He felt that the high tax rate of California was driving business away. He then advocated stricter law enforcement, including the death penalty for drug dealers.

Nixon spoke at some length about his opponent being soft on Communism. Nixon had a long history of anti-Communist politics during the McCarthy era. He had been an early member of the House Un-American Activities Committee, who had a role in the now infamous "Hollywood blacklist" in which entertainment figures were denied employment based only on rumors or suspicion of Communist sympathies. Nixon had built his career on the pursuit of Communist sympathizers, most famously in the Alger Hiss case.

In his speech in Montrose, he continued that line of thought by advocating stringent investigation of suspected Communists. He specifically vowed to introduce legislation to bar the free speech on college campuses of anyone who refused to answer questions about their Communist affiliations.

Nixon then took a tour of the local newspaper's offices and printing presses. During an interview with the paper's editor, he expressed support for Max Rafferty, another very conservative public figure, who was leaving his position as head of the La Cañada School District for a successful run at the state superintendent of public instruction. Nixon's "attractive and intelligent wife" Pat also showed interest in that race.

Soon after the tour, the Nixon motorcade left Montrose for its next stop in Glendale "in a wake of waving banners and pandemonium" as the newspaper described it.

Despite Nixon's warm reception in Montrose, he did not win that race for governor for several reasons. There was the obvious uphill battle against a relatively popular incumbent. Also, Nixon's "communist conspiracy" platform did not resonate with voters. But more importantly, voters recognized that his run for governor was in fact an attempt to position himself for another run for president. After his defeat, he delivered the iconic sour-grapes speech, "You won't have Nixon to kick around anymore". But as most readers know, we did indeed have Nixon to kick around again in 1974, when he resigned the presidency in the face of impeachment.

The Great Tujunga Canyon Train Wreck

A train wreck in Big Tujunga Canyon? But is there even a railroad there?

Well, there was a short set of tracks along with a locomotive and some cars for a few weeks in 1942, in support of the movie *The Spoilers*. This quasi-western actually set in the Alaskan gold rush starred John Wayne, Marlene Dietrich, and Randolph Scott. It follows the exploits of a group of Alaskan gold miners beset by claim jumpers. John Wayne, playing his classic he-man character, portrays a successful miner who is being swindled out of his mine by a group of con men. The con men are led by Randolph Scott portraying a villain, a role he rarely played. Marlene Dietrich plays the tough saloon owner who has fallen hard for John Wayne. There is a fun but brief cameo with the actual poet Robert W. Service, in which the saloon owner asks him about his poem "The Shooting of Dan McGrew." John Wayne battles the con men for his mine, during which this train crash takes place. The film culminates in an epic fist-fight between Wayne and Randolph Scott. The athletic brawl is one of the longest in film history, lasting an amazing four minutes. That fight alone is worth watching the movie.

But for us here in the Crescenta Valley the wow factor of the movie is the very obvious Big Tujunga Canyon background to many of the scenes. Filming of interior shots and action in the goldrush boomtown were at Universal Studios, but the mining camp and train set was in Big Tujunga Canyon.

In his book *Growing Up in Sunland*, Tom Gilfoy describes the movie set he saw as a young boy:

> The set was elaborate with dozens of buildings and miner's tents scattered across the wash from the foot of Oro Vista Avenue all the way to the cliffs where the bridge to Riverwood Ranch now crosses the stream. A false entrance to a goldmine was dug into the cliffs near this same bridge. Several hundred yards of railroad track were laid, and an old steam locomotive and ore cars were trucked in for the movie's biggest scene.

In the movie, the full-size locomotive races down the short track, hits a barricade, rolls over on its side, and skids to a stop, hissing steam. This was before CGI, so they actually had to wreck a real train, right there in "Big T" Canyon.

The narrow-gauge locomotive used in the movie has a story of its own. It was built in 1875 for the Carson and Tahoe Lumber Company, and later transferred to the Nevada County Narrow-Gauge. But in 1940, the old steam engine with the classic funnel-shaped smokestack was picked up by Universal Studios for use in the many westerns being filmed. It was featured in over 100 movies and TV shows, including *Winchester '73*, *The Virginian*, and *Alias Smith and Jones*. In 1985, Universal Studios saw less of a need for the old locomotive and acquiesced to the pleas of the Nevada County Narrow-Gauge Railway Museum to bring the "little teakettle on wheels" home to Nevada County in Northern California. It's apparently under restoration currently.

The author found the movie more entertaining that most westerns of that era, mostly because of the Big Tujunga Canyon location shots and the train wreck, but for many other reasons as well, such as the epic fight scene, I mentioned earlier. The wide cast of classic character actors is delightful, including Harry Carey and host of other recognizable faces. As WWII had just begun, Marlene Dietrich makes a clumsy effort to squash her German accent, which comes off pretty funny. The political incorrectness of the movie is way over the top, with numerous scenes of racial degradation and sexual impropriety. In what other movie can you see John Wayne in both blackface and wearing women's clothing? The best feature for me though were the thick layer-upon-layer of double entendre and sexual innuendo in the dialog.

Shown here is a shot from the 1942 John Wayne movie *The Spoilers*. In the movie, this is supposed to be a mining camp in Alaska, but in reality, it is Big Tujunga Canyon. A train owned by Universal Studios chugs alongside the streambed. The vegetation is still sparse from having been stripped out by the 1938 flood. (*YouTube*)

The Spoilers (the 1942 version, there are others) can be seen on the IMDB channel. It is a delight and was filmed right in our backyard.

Mysterious Woman "Lost" In Pickens Canyon

This story showed up in old newspapers—a simple story of a woman lost in the mountains above C.V. Yet the more one reads, the odder it seems. In January 1948, Mr. and Mrs. William Reed of 5725 Canyonside Road, high up on Briggs Terrace, were hosting their niece, thirty-year-old Alberta Royal McCreery for the holidays. Alberta had come to L.A. from a small town in Illinois and was living in Hollywood, working as a dress designer. The papers described her as diminutive and pretty, and she was said to be an "outdoorsy type."

On Thursday, January 8, the Reeds found a note from Alberta, stating simply that she "was going into the hills." The Reeds were not concerned as she had hiked the area many times, but she did not return that night, so the next day, the Reeds reported her missing at the Montrose Sheriff Station. Sheriff's cars began their search. As Friday wore on with no trace of the woman, the Mounted Sheriff Posse (precursor of the Montrose

Search and Rescue team) was called in. Sheriffs on horseback began to search the trails of the San Gabriels. As the weekend wore on, the search intensified, and over 100 volunteers were combing the mountains.

This was turning into a big deal. The search was hitting the front pages of national newspapers. Terms like "hope fades" and "futile search" were peppering the news stories. Reports came in of buzzards circling the mountainside. The major disaster unit at the sheriff station was mobilized, a Red Cross HQ was opened, and a bloodhound from Folsom Prison was brought in. A plane was chartered to search the mountains. The tiny Montrose Sheriff Station became a beehive of activity as fifteen extra sheriffs crowded in to chase down leads, and the leads were coming in.

Sightings of her were reported everywhere. A cab driver reported that he picked up a young woman in La Crescenta on Thursday night, and that she had him drive her around aimlessly all night, finally dropping her off in Long Beach. A man reported that he sat next to a troubled woman on a bus ride to Yuma who matched her description perfectly. Other details came from her family. She had been on an extreme juice fast for ten days before her disappearance. She was extremely depressed because of a failed romance. By Monday, the family and the sheriff were both saying they believed she was somewhere other than the mountains.

But on Tuesday morning, a lone searcher started up the trail on the Ocean View side of Pickens immediately across the canyon from the Reeds home. He had just passed an abandoned cabin that had been searched several times already, when he came on Alberta, sitting by the side of the trail, within sight of the Reed house. She seemed fine, fresh in fact, and told the man that she had no idea that everyone was looking for her. The two walked the quarter mile down into Pickens Canyon and up the other side to the Reed house where the media converged on Alberta.

She coyly posed for the newsmen's cameras, smiling, confident, and surprisingly clean. She told reporters that she had decided to spend some time alone. Dressed in slacks, a blouse, and light jacket, she said she had grabbed a blanket and a couple of oranges and grapefruits and had spent the five January nights alternately in the abandoned cabin across from the Reed home, and further up the trail on the ground, wrapped in the blanket. She seemed surprised that she was considered missing, seeing as she had left the note. She claimed to have not seen any of the many search parties. One of her friends tried to shut down the news interviews to protect Alberta's privacy, but she shot back, "I'm a free soul—I talk to whom I please." Alberta insisted she had been in the mountains the entire time.

In a check of the papers, I looked for a follow up story on this mystery, but none appears. The story sounds suspicious, and there must be more to it, but we will just have to wonder.

Two weeks after I published this story for a column in the local paper, one of my readers sent me Alberta's obituary. It turns out she died just before I wrote the account. Apparently, after her adventures in California, she returned to the Midwest. She never married but became a favorite aunt to her family and an adored member of the community. She was a musician and was very spiritual. Her family had never heard this story, so perhaps she wanted this incident hidden. She died at just the time that I got the idea to write her story. I wonder if her spirit was reaching out to finally have that story told?

6
Weird Nature

The Parrots of Crescenta Valley

Many wild animals have adapted and even flourished in our increasingly urban Foothills community—coyotes, raccoons, possums, and hawks—but there is one non-native wild species that seemingly defies credulity for surviving and thriving in the Crescenta Valley: wild parrots.

The author first noticed them about ten years ago, a small flock feasting on Juniper berries in the trees along our property line. As a Southern California native, I had always been aware of their existence in Pasadena and the San Gabriel Valley. I was surprised they had made it over this far, believing the old urban legend that they were a single flock that was released from a burning pet store in the 1950s. Since then, I have noticed their relentless spread through the urban jungles of L.A. and have read that they thrive by the thousands all over California, and many other places in the nation for that matter. They thrive everywhere except, ironically, their native Mexico, where parrot poachers have destroyed much of their habitat in order to smuggle them to—guess where—here. Those that are studying the emerging local parrot population say that our current lineup of some thirteen different established species of parrots and parakeets point to escapees from those smugglers as the source for the wide variety of tropical birds, rather than the more colorful "fire in a pet store" legend. Macaws, cockatoos, African greys, cockatiels, and budgies are also spotted in L.A., but they do not seem yet to have established themselves into flocks.

As springtime kicks in, parrots are seen foraging across our valley in greater numbers. Their food source is what we traditionally grow in our yards and in retail landscaping, such as date palms, fruit trees and berries, nuts and seeds, and even some flowers. The normal decorative plants we take for granted are a feast for the parrots. They have a complex social structure and check in with one another on a nearly constant basis with distinctive squawks, constantly repeating "I'm here! My name is Polly! I'm here!" kind of like a very loud form of Facebook. Each evening, the parrots find a tree to spend the night in and engage in an ear-splitting hour or so of sorting themselves into amiable groups for the night's sleep. Bright and early the next morning, they noisily reform into "who they want to fly next to" and begin their morning commute to their first meal of the day.

As their numbers have shot up into the thousands in the last few years, urban wildlife experts and ornithologists have created "The California Parrot Project" based out of the Natural History Museum downtown. They are tracking the spread of this tropical phenomenon, studying them in true scientific fashion. Their website www.californiaparrotproject.org provides a guide to identify the different species, gives some background on them, and, if you care to participate, provides a form to send in sightings so they can monitor the parrots' expanding range.

The parrots are beautiful to look at and provide an exotic flavor to our neighborhoods, but they can be noisy (to put it mildly) if you happen to live under one of their evening "sorting out" trees, not to mention the resulting mess left by a hundred parrots when they leave in the morning. Perhaps more worrisome to wild bird lovers is that parrots may crowd out native birds, competing for nesting spots and food sources as their population explodes. Parrots have few natural predators, and our hawks don't seem to know what to do with them. Like it or not, they will become an increasingly familiar part of La Crescenta.

Some C.V. residents may welcome the parrots, and others will not, and sometimes attitudes are surprising. Even some fanatical animal lovers I know have reservations about them—that they are loud and aggressive, and force the natives out. I say that makes them just like us.

The War of the Black Widow Spiders

Our valley has a near perfect climate, and as such attracts newcomers from all over the world. Besides the human newcomers, foreign plant and animal life also does well here, so-called "invasive species".

To anyone growing up in the Crescenta Valley, the black widow spider was legendary. To kids, they seemingly lurked under every rock, piece of wood, unused toy or play equipment. Our garages seemed alive with them, and in our over-active young minds, they hunted children. They were evil-looking and deadly. Just a touch would result in agonizing death.

Like most of our childhood lore, the reality is quite a bit milder. Widow spiders are worldwide, in various colorations. Our local widow, the western black widow, has the distinctive shiny black body with the iconic red hourglass on its belly. The bite, which we as kids considered deadly, is hardly so. Almost no one has ever died from the bite of a western black widow, and the worst that can be expected is muscle pain or cramping for a few days. Many that are bitten get no symptoms at all, as the spider does not always inject venom with its bite. Even the name black widow is a slight exaggeration. In the wild, the female almost never eats the male after mating. That generalization came from observing captive black widow mating, where the male was trapped in a container, and couldn't escape. In the wild, the male is always careful to make sure the female has just eaten before approaching them, and he beats a hasty retreat after the act. By the way, the term for this behavior is "sexual cannibalism," which is a wonderfully underused metaphor for some human behavior.

The black widow has been prolific all these years, but that began to change in 2002. That year, the L.A. County Museum of Natural History was conducting an urban spider survey. On an outreach trip to a Torrance elementary school, a kid brought over a brown spider on a leaf. The entomologist recognized it as a widow, but she had not seen that type before. She took it back to the lab where it was identified as a brown widow spider. The entomologists knew this native of Africa had been popping up in other parts of the world, but this was the first time it had been observed here. Returning to the school, they found brown widows everywhere—under the school-ground benches, on the chain-link around the school, and in the play equipment.

It caused a sensation in Torrance, but remained localized there for a couple of years. Soon however, the brown widow population exploded, and they began showing up in big numbers all over L.A. and San Diego. As their numbers went up, the numbers of the native western black widow went down.

The brown widows have basically the same behavior as the classic black widows. They nest in the same spots and compete for the same food. The difference is that browns reproduce about twice as fast as the blacks. Plus, the babies spread faster due to a behavior called "ballooning"—they throw out a bit of web like a kite which catches any light breeze, and they are lifted to ride to a new location.

The quickly reproducing brown widow spider (*desertusa.com*)

How to identify brown widows? They are shaped like blacks and have the distinctive hourglass on the abdomen. However, on browns, the hourglass is orange and is not as pronounced against the brown body, and the legs are tan with darker stripes.

The bad news is that the browns are quickly displacing the blacks, and the blacks will soon be rare. The good news is brown widows are much less venomous, and bites are only slightly worse that a regular household spider bite. As this population shift takes hold, cleaning out one's garage or bringing in firewood will no longer have the thrill of danger it once had.

What the Heck Happened to Our Horny Toads?

Before video games, children spent hours hunting lizards in the many vacant lots in C.V. It was strictly catch-and-release, mind you. The point was the thrill of the chase, a brief moment of triumph while the panic-stricken lizard tried to squirm out of kids' dirty hands, and then the escape back to the omnipresent rock piles. Blue-bellies (western fence lizard) and fierce alligator lizards made up the bulk of the catch, but the most sought-after prey was the prehistoric-looking "horny toad."

Horny toads, actually called "horned lizards," have a range throughout Western North America. More than a dozen different species exist, but in our area, the coast horned

The horned lizard or "horny toad." (*californiaherps.com*)

lizard dominates. The horned toad is the most charismatic of the local lizards, due in part to their resemblance to cartoon dinosaurs. They are flat and round, their bodies covered in short spikes. A wide crown or collar of longer spikes around their blunt heads completes their fearsome appearance. If this were not fantastical enough, they can squirt a small amount of blood from their eyes a couple of feet when threatened. Despite all these seemingly horrifying descriptions, they are actually endearing in a "so ugly, they're cute" sort of way.

However, about twenty years ago, this interesting little lizard that could be found in any backyard in the valley seemingly disappeared. Despite there being no shortage of other lizards, the horny toad population has collapsed, so much so that they are on the verge of being declared an endangered species. Their particular lizard dynasty was destroyed by a small problem (very small)—the Argentine ant.

The Argentine ant is the basic black ant that we are all familiar with, but they are not from around here—they are invasive. In the 1890s, a little colony of Argentine ants came in to California from South America with a load of coffee or sugar. This small colony has expanded into a single massive colony that incredibly now encompasses nearly the entire state. Our native ants spend a good amount of their time competing with other native ant colonies, even those of the same species. The Argentine ant however, because they belong to a single massive colony, does not compete with other Argentine ants, and instead focuses their collective energies on destroying the native colonies. They are incredibly efficient at this and have entirely eliminated the native ants in some areas. For those familiar with Star Trek terminology, Argentine ants are the Borg, and for native ants, "Resistance is futile."

Why is this a problem for the horny toad? Their diet is almost entirely ants, but they hate Argentine ants. They will eat them if they have to, but they cannot thrive on a diet of only Argentine ants. Biologists experimenting with horny toads found that diets of exclusively Argentine ants caused weight loss and decline in the lizards. Apparently, the ants do not contain the right nutrients. Not only are Argentine ants multiplying and destroying the horny toad's food source, but now a fire ant invasion is occurring. Fire ants can actually attack and bring down small animals, posing an ecological nightmare for horned lizards. Combine this with loss of habitat (more parking lots and housing developments), and the horny toads might soon be a thing of the past.

Not to be all doom and gloom, Argentine ants need more water than California can naturally supply, and a drier state means less Argentine ants. Biological surveys have shown that wildfire burn areas show a resurgence in native ant populations and a corresponding resurgence in the horny toad numbers. Recently, one native ant population in Northern California actually developed a chemical secretion that kills invasive Argentine ants. You can never predict the twists and turns of natural selection.

Alligator Lizards

The alligator lizard is quite common today. They are ever present in backyards, often hiding under foliage or debris, other times sunning on a rock.

The alligator lizard has a long snake-like body, with small, short legs that almost seem an afterthought. Nine to thirteen dark bands run across their backs and tails, with the areas between the bands a yellow, orange or grey. Their scales are keeled, or ridged in the center, making them feel rough to the touch. They are commonly in the 5–8-inch range, but can grow up to 16 inches long. The head of the alligator lizard is very snake-like in appearance, and they have large yellow eyes.

Their tails are extraordinarily long—twice the length of their bodies. Like many other lizards, they have a unique and fascinating self-defense mechanism in the form of a tail that will automatically detach when grasped by a predator. Anything chasing an alligator lizard is likely to grab its extraordinarily long tail first. Naturally occurring fracture planes in the tail provide weak spots where the tail can easily break cleanly off. The detached tail will immediately go into a wild spasm, thrashing around and distracting the predator enough to allow the now tailless lizard to slink away unnoticed. Sphincter muscles in the lizard end of the tail stump squeeze off blood flow, and a new tail will grow back after a few weeks. It is not unusual to spot a "stumpy" alligator lizard, or one in which the tail has grown back in a slightly different color.

Although they have defenses against higher level predators, they are excellent predators themselves. They eat any other creature smaller than themselves—a wide spectrum of insects (including black widow spiders), baby birds and bird eggs, even other alligator lizards. Woodpiles are a favored spot for alligator lizards because of the black widows that often hide there. Alligator lizard mating is a brutish affair in which the male grabs the female's head in his powerful jaws and holds her immobile until she submits.

Although they are active all year, they are encountered most often in springtime when people are clearing weeds or prepping the garden. If you catch one, they will sometimes try to bite you, just like their namesake the alligator, but it's a painless bite. Be sure to let them go again so they will eat the pests in your yard. Since they live ten to fifteen years, you are likely to spot the same one over and over. Alligator lizards are a friend to man, and a benefit to every garden.

Our Local Bats

In summer, it is easy to spot bats flying in the evening sky. After the sun goes down, but before it is fully dark, fast black blurs can be made out against the sky, darting quickly this way and that, as they grab flying insects in mid-air. They are social, helpful to man, and are critical to the ecosystem, yet they are misunderstood and often maligned. Many fear them as blood suckers or carriers of rabies, but the truth is they do nothing but good for us. A single brown bat, one of the more common bats locally, is eating up to 500 mosquitos an hour as they flitter about in the dark. Imagine what life would be like without them.

There are about twenty-seven different varieties of bats in the L.A. area. They live a long time, as long as thirty years. They are not rodents; they are more closely related to dogs and horses.

As we all know, bats hunt bugs with echolocation. They squeak out a high-pitch sound, which bounces off the flying insect, and returns to the bat—an echo. They determine the direction of the insect by the direction of the echo and take off after them.

Bats often have bizarre looking faces and ears, with strange wrinkles and protrusions, giving them a fierce alien look. The bat's ugly faces are actually designed to channel the returning echo into their ears.

The squeak they use for echolocation is at such a high frequency that the human ear cannot hear it, and that is a good thing because those squeaks are phenomenally loud—as high as 140 decibels. The threshold of pain for human ears is 120 decibels. If those squeaks were in the frequency range of human hearing, we would have to wear ear protection at night.

Bats are not blind. Their eyesight is as good as ours. They seem to use their eyesight for flying and echolocation for hunting the tiny bugs their eyes would miss—a cooperative venture between the two senses.

In spring, they form maternity colonies to help cooperatively with raising their pups. They have (usually) one baby at a time and nurture them. They are mammals so they produce milk for their young. If disturbed, they will carry their young away to safety. If a member of the colony is injured, the others will feed them.

Since we don't have a lot of "bat caves" around here for bats to sleep in during the day, they mainly sleep in trees and sometimes under the eaves of houses or in rock crevasses on the hillsides.

Although none live around here, a few species of bats eat nectar like hummingbirds, and like hummingbirds and bees, they pollenate a wide variety of plants. Bats are primary pollinators for cocoa plants that produces chocolate and agave that produces tequila—thank you bats.

Bats are a fun part of summer evenings, entertaining to watch. They have adapted well to our urban environment. If you would like to view bats, head outside on one of our warm, still summer evenings. Although you can often see them right in front your home, heading out to where there are bodies of water, such as Devils Gate Dam, is a good bet. There are more mosquitos there. They are also attracted to the insects that congregate at night around the big floodlights commonly found on athletic fields. To enhance the experience, "bat detectors" can be purchased. These fairly inexpensive handheld devices will pick up the inaudible high-frequency calls of bats and convert them to audible sound levels, some devices even identifying the species of bats and whether they are feeding or just communicating. Many models exist that are dedicated units, while an increasing number are apps for smartphones with receiver attachments that plug into your phone.

Next time you see bats darting around the sky of a hot summer evening, think about the great service they do us. Our summer nights would be pretty miserable without them. Thank bats for the mosquito bites you do not have.

Yes, We Have Native Bees

While we are all familiar with the non-native classic honey bee we see buzzing about our gardens, there is a whole other world of native bees that we do not even notice, buzzing around those same flowers. There are about 1,600 different varieties here in California that vary so much in shape, color, and size that many are unrecognizable as bees.

While we usually think of bees in terms of honey, the reality is that pollination is their major function. Agriculture would literally fail without bee pollination. Pollinating bees are absolutely vital to man's survival. Although native bees do not produce harvestable honey, they do a much better job of pollinating than honey bees. In fact, they pollinate many food plants that honey bees do poorly with, such as alfalfa, melons, cranberries, blueberries, soybeans, and sunflowers. Some plants like tomato, potato, and eggplant are mainly pollinated by something called "buzz-pollination," which can only be done by native bees. In a scenario that sounds fantastic, native bees position themselves under a flower and begin to vibrate or buzz, hitting around 400 Hz. Once they hit exactly the right pitch, the plant vibrates in resonance and dumps a load of pollen on the bee—honey bees cannot do this.

Native bees have so far been resistant to the much-publicized bee die-off or colony collapse that is affecting the world's honey bee population. As well, native bees do not compete with honey bees, and *vice versa*. While non-native honey bees are social, the majority of native bees are solitary. They live alone, laying eggs in holes in the ground or in dead wood, and feed their young with the pollen they collect, rather than making honey.

On a recent native bee expedition at Deukmejian Park, a bee expert took us outside to find some native bees. Standing beside a flowering bush, we saw hundreds of honey bees. Yet looking closer, we began to notice smaller, darker bees among the crowd, bees that in the past would have been dismissed as young bees. These were one variety of native bees.

Next, we were buzzed by one of those big black bumble bees—the carpenter bee. This is another native bee, and a buzz-pollinator as well. With a fine mesh net, the guide then collected a few native bees for a close-up look. One bee they caught was a bright green metallic color, looking nothing like a bee. Another was literally the size of a gnat. As a sideline, they snatched up a couple of flies that are camouflaged to look like bees for self-protection.

So get out in your yard and watch the bees. Now look a little closer, past those normal bees—you will discover a whole new world of native bees.

Band-Tailed Pigeon: Our Only True Native Pigeon

The author and his wife have found immense joy in the bird feeder we set up a few years ago. It hangs on a rope from the eaves right outside a big picture window in our living room, perfect for observing the ebb and flow of migrating species, along with our resident birds. We have struggled to keep our bird feeder from becoming a squirrel feeder, and have found amusement in the intelligent rodents' efforts to overcome the squirrel-guards. We also get an occasional dose of the "circle of life" when a hawk or falcon makes a pass through.

By far the most spectacular bird that visits is our native-Californian band-tailed pigeon. They are huge, nearly the size of a chicken. They are much too big to fit on the narrow feeding trough. They always come in pairs, landing on a branch a few feet from the feeder. They examine the logistics of the situation for a couple minutes, weighing the difficulty of the landing on the too-small ledge to the temptation of a free meal. Often the braver of the pair will flap over and land sideways on the trough edge, flapping the outboard wing wildly to stay upright, while grabbing mouthfuls of seed. This sets the suspended bird feeder to start slowly rotating. The second bird will then join the first, also landing sideways on the opposite side, and flapping its outer-facing wing. Now the feeder starts spinning faster and faster from their wings flapping, until finally centrifugal force spins them off.

When we think of pigeons, we usually think of the common urban pigeon or rock pigeon. They are not native and were introduced to America from Europe in the 1600s. They are smaller than our native band-tailed pigeon, but do bear a resemblance, as does the mourning dove.

The native band-tailed pigeon is easily identified by its size, as long as 16 inches and beefy, weighing over 1 lb. They are grey with a white band on the back of the neck. When seen up close, they have an iridescent sheen on their necks of green and pink—very pretty. The clincher for ready identification is that their beaks and legs are bright yellow-orange. They are gentle, sweet and sociable, and have a soft low call similar to an owl.

Band-tailed pigeons prefer foothills and mountains, oak woodlands like our areas. They inhabit the Pacific coastal mountains and parts of the southwest. Some flocks migrate, others stay in place year-round. Their natural feed is acorns and elderberries, but they obviously also visit bird feeders for seeds. As well, they can feed on introduced fruits and seeds. The widespread planting of English holly and common ivy have attracted them into suburban eras like ours.

They are most closely related to the storied but extinct passenger pigeon. The passenger pigeon once blackened the skies by the millions, but were hunted to complete extinction by Americans in the late 1800s. The same fate almost befell our band-tailed pigeons. They were hunted extensively here in the west, and by the turn of the century, they were becoming scarce. Hunting was put on hold, but unlike the passenger pigeon, they rebounded, and today offer hunting sport in a limited capacity.

However, their biggest threat today is disease. A particular bacterium, *avian trichomonosis*, has plagued the band-tailed pigeon for decades and occasionally flairs up as it did in 2007 and 2015. I was horrified to read that experts were recommending removing bird feeders to slow the spread of the disease. I would hate to lose my bird feeder. My guilt was assuaged when I read that transmission of the bacteria occurs when band-tailed pigeons and rock pigeons (common urban pigeons) share a common feeder. Rock pigeons are carriers. Fortunately, we have very few common pigeons here in the valley, and none at my feeder.

We have so many things of natural beauty here in Crescenta Valley. The band-tailed pigeon is one beautiful native bird we are lucky to share our valley with. I get great joy when these massive birds set my bird feeder to spinning.

C.V. is the Front Line of the Squirrel Wars

The Crescenta Valley is currently the front line in yet another battle between a native species and invasive species. In this case, it is the native western gray squirrel versus the invasive eastern fox squirrel. While the invasive fox squirrels occupy the valley, the native gray squirrels are waging a holding action from the edges of the mountains, slowly being pushed back by the aggressive invaders.

The native gray squirrel once roamed the oak woodlands and pine forests of Southern California unchallenged. Yet in the late 1800s, an "Old Soldiers Home" was established in West Los Angeles (today's VA Hospital). Civil War vets were used to eating squirrels in their eastern homes, and when they retired to L.A., they brought their eastern fox squirrel "pets" with them for an occasional squirrel stew. By the turn of the century, many fox squirrels had escaped the menu at the Old Soldiers Home and were spreading tree to tree in the orchards of the L.A. basin. As the oak woodlands were replaced with walnut orchards, and then housing tracts with fruit trees in the yards, the fox squirrels' territory expanded with the spreading suburbia. It turns out that just like coyotes, raccoons and possums, the eastern fox squirrel was readily adaptable to an urban environment. The native gray squirrels are not, and as the city spreads, they have retreated further into the hills. In just over a century, the eastern fox squirrel has become the most common squirrel in Los Angeles, and their range now extends from Orange County to Simi Valley, and from Palos Verdes, west all the way to the Crescenta Valley. Recently, the expansion has accelerated as urban homeowners live-trap the pesky fox squirrels in "Have-a-hart" traps, and transport them to L.A.'s fringes for release. In the metaphor of "squirrel wars," they are like paratroopers being dropped behind enemy lines.

Which squirrel do you have in your yard? Visually, the two look similar. The native western gray is truly gray with a white underbelly. They are found generally on the fringes of the valley, up against the San Gabriels on Briggs Terrace, or among the oak groves that line the edges of the Verdugo Mountains. The invasive eastern fox squirrel has more brown in the fur, even slightly reddish, and is found in the built out areas of C.V. Behavior-wise, the two are slightly different. The western gray is shyer, whereas the eastern fox tends to be aggressive, opportunistic and, well, pesky. The western gray eats exclusively acorns and pine nuts, while the eastern fox squirrel eats almost anything, from acorns, to fruit, to old pizza crusts, making them well adapted to urbanization. Not only that, but the eastern fox squirrel reproduces twice as fast as the native grays, their continuing expansion being assured by sheer numbers alone.

So where is this war headed? Why can they not "all just get along"? Seemly they do in some areas. Fern Dell in Griffith Park for instance has gray and fox squirrels living in harmony side-by-side. The native grays have even been observed mating with the eastern fox squirrels, although no hybrid offspring have been seen. Yet research has shown that as resources become strained, the more adaptable and faster reproducing eastern fox squirrel will push out the native grays. It is not just here. All across the western states, introduced eastern fox squirrels are gaining footholds and expanding their range, as human homes are being built further into once wild areas. It appears that the eastern fox squirrel's territory will continue to expand as man's continues to expand.

There will probably always be native gray squirrels in our preserved areas—the Verdugo Mountains and the Angeles Forest. Perhaps the squirrel wars will stabilize into a "cold war" with political boundaries that do not move. And the consequences of this change in squirrel species? Probably little, if any. It is just another little-noticed chapter in the long story of man's influence on nature.

Orange Spaghetti? Silly String? UFO Droppings? What is It?!

You have seen it, and no doubt wondered what the heck it is—tangles of bright yellow or orange string that cover plants, usually out in the chaparral, but sometimes in your yard as well. It looks like someone sprayed the plants with some kind of orange plastic. Indeed, if you touch it, the plant has a decidedly plastic feel to it. Surprisingly, it is not some weird invasive species—it is a California native. Its actual name is cuscuta and is

Cuscuta, sometimes called dodder, does not look like a California native, although it is. It does not even look like it comes from this planet. (*baynature.org*)

commonly referred to as dodder, but it has many wildly descriptive nicknames: devil's guts, devil's hair, devil's ringlet, goldthread, hairweed, hellbine, love vine, pull-down, strangleweed, angel hair, and witch's hair.

Cuscuta's appearance is distinctly alien, but its growth methods are even more other-worldly. Like many classic aliens in science fiction, it's parasitic. It comes up from seed as a 2–4-inch thread, which will grow towards plants around it, looking for a suitable host to latch onto. The seedling can sense the prospects of the available host plants, and will grow toward the plants with the greatest amount of moisture and nutrients. It will ignore inanimate objects. Recent experiments have shown that it somehow "smells" suitable hosts. The stem "gropes" through the air until it makes contact, then quickly takes a couple of wraps around the host branch. Once it has a good hold, it then begins to grow sharp appendages (like roots) that penetrate the flesh of the host plant. It is from these insertions into the plant's vascular system that the cuscuta will draw its water and nutrients. The cuscuta then disconnects from its ground roots and begins growing up its host plant at a rate of nearly 3 inches a day, sometimes entirely covering the host (victim?).

It does not photosynthesize like normal plants, but instead gets all its nutrients from its host. Although it does not kill its host outright, it can weaken it enough to make it susceptible to disease. If cuscuta is attached to more than one plant it can spread disease as well. As it does not use photosynthesis, it has no chlorophyll, which is the chemical that makes plants green—thus its unnatural color. In the early summer, the by then well-established cuscuta develops small flowers, then even tinier seeds, which drop to the ground in large quantities, thus making it an annually returning plant. The seeds are hardy and can survive five years until the right conditions for germination are reached. We tend to see cuscuta in the wild chaparral where it is just a novelty, but in agriculture, particularly the alfalfa fields of California's high desert, cuscuta is a real problem. Up to 90 percent of the fields have an infestation problem, and mowing or burning the affected areas is often the only solution.

Our local Native Americans used cuscuta as a cure for black-widow bites, but they only used cuscuta that had grown on buckwheat. Apparently, the buckwheat introduced certain critical chemicals into the cuscuta. Other medicinal uses by the Natives include poultices for treatment of bruises and insect bites, and cuscuta baths for tuberculosis. This use translated to the white man, and early settlers used this cure as well. The Chinese also used cuscuta medicinally.

Cuscuta is found worldwide, in all the temperate and tropical zones, in 170 different species, all of them white, yellow, orange, and even red in color. In California, it is prevalent in all areas from sea level to over 8,000 feet. It is related to the morning glory, although some call it a fungus rather than a plant.

So next time you are out, note the orange patches on our chaparral covered hills. If you can, get your hands on it to experience its weird texture. This mysterious growth, with its seeming near-intelligence and its alien nature is by far our strangest native plant.

Another of Our Weirdest Native Plants: The Wild Cucumber

But next in line as strangest native plant would be the wild cucumber. Those venturing out onto our local trails in late winter/early spring are bound to notice light-green vines growing out across the trails and climbing up into the surrounding chaparral. Walk the same trail the next day and the vines will be twice as long—they grow that fast. In just a few weeks, these vines will produce fruit that are one of the weirder sights you will see in our mountains: nasty little green orbs covered in scary-looking spikes. They have a distinctly alien look, and they look startlingly out of place. Yet they are not—they are a California native: the wild cucumber.

Like many native plants, the wild cucumber is known by several names, some with interesting origins. "Cucumber" because in some of its variations throughout the western states the fruit is less spikey, and does look a little cucumber-like. It is also called "manroot" or "old man in the ground." That is because the vines grow from a perennial tuber, or root, that gets huge with age, sometimes over 100 lb. This large root divides into "legs" and looks vaguely human when dug up. The plant's real name is "Marah," after a Biblical place

In late winter and spring, the very weird-looking wild cucumber can be easily found in our mountains, and unfortunately sometimes in our yards as well. (*growitbuildit.com*)

name mentioned in Exodus, where the Moses-led Israelites came to a well where the water was too bitter to drink. The plant is indeed extremely bitter to the taste, thus the name.

The huge tuber slumbers underground through the summer and fall, dormant, but after the first rain of winter, the vines explode up out of the ground and take off in every direction. Its strategy is to take advantage of the short-term abundance of water and grow as fast as it can. It quickly pushes out a few leaves for photosynthesis and some small white flowers for reproduction. As some flowers are male and others female, it self-germinates. The fruit—the "cucumbers"—develop quickly, and after the last rain of our short rainy season, the plant goes dormant again. The vines dry up, and the spikey fruit turns yellow, then tan in color. The seeds drop out of the dried-up cucumbers, which are generally eaten by various birds and animals. Yet the strength of the plant is stored in the huge underground tuber. The vines can be cut off, year after year, as they often are near trails, and they just keep coming back from the stored energy in the root. It survives fires as well, and is often the first plant to re-appear.

Although the plants, fruit and seeds are inedible, even poisonous to humans, the local Native Americans, who used everything in their natural world, found uses for wild cucumber. The vines and fruit were mashed into poultices and soaking solutions for various ailments. The tuber was used as soap. Some tribes mashed the fruit and root, and placed it in streams. The wild cucumber contains a chemical that apparently denies oxygen to fish in the stream, stunning them, and causing them to float to the surface. The roots and seeds were also used by the Indians as a purgative. This seems to be the only use the white man picked up. California wild cucumber was the active ingredient in Stoughton's Bitters, a popular laxative of the nineteenth century. Of course, there is the notorious rumor that is applied to so many native plants—that the plant has hallucinogenic properties. As the plant is somewhat poisonous, it seems a pretty risky high.

In most of the U.S., winter is a time of bare plants and brown ground cover. The plants come alive in spring and stay brilliant green all summer from the frequent summer rains. Here in Southern California, it is just the opposite. Many native plants take advantage of our short winter rains with a growth spurt, then hunker down and try to survive the coming several months of no rain. So as you venture out onto our local trails, say hello to the prickly wild cucumber, a true California native plant, and one that reflects so well our seemingly backward natural growing season.

Ailanthus: Tree of Heaven, or Tree from Hell?

The Ailanthus tree is becoming one of the most common growths found in La Crescenta. It comes up in vacant lots, along sidewalks and roadways, and is symbiotic with development, as it prefers disturbed soil to sprout. Once you learn to recognize it, you begin to realize how prevalent it actually is. It is a tall, slender, grey-barked tree. The leaves are most distinctive, growing on long red-brown stems, each holding ten or twenty leaves. It is deciduous, and the leaves turn yellow before falling. The plant has a strong sharp nutty odor when cut or when you rub your fingers on the leaves. It propagates both by seeds and underground runners, and if left unchecked will quickly form dense thickets. It may be the fastest growing tree in North America, up to 6 feet a year, and can reach 80 feet.

Ailanthus Altissima is known by many nicknames. Most common is "Tree of Heaven" or "Chinese Sumac," but is also known as "Stinking Sumac," "Tree from Hell," and "Ghetto Palm" (for its tendency to grow in abandoned urban areas). The 1943 novel, turned movie, turned musical *A Tree Grows in Brooklyn* refers to the Ailanthus tree, common in New York's poorer neighborhoods. The tree serves as a metaphor for the immigrant class as it grows up through cement sidewalks, rubbish heaps and sewer grates. It thrives wherever its seeds land. Like New York's immigrant class, it is tough, resilient, and needs no cultivation.

Ailanthus has a long history of interaction with man. It is native to China, where it is an important symbol in their mythology and literature. Ailanthus was a common ornamental tree in the Orient and was used to feed silkworms for silk production. It is a vital component in Chinese medicine, treating a wide variety of ailments including

A small sample of the hundreds of ailanthus trees growing in the vacant lot at Foothill and Sunset, where a house was torn down. They love disturbed soil, and any effort to cut one down will just result in even more growing in its place. (*Author*)

epilepsy, mental illness, and baldness. It was imported to Europe in the 1740s and then to America in 1784, where it was prized as garden tree. It was a common street tree all across the U.S. up into the early part of this century. A century after it was introduced on the East Coast, it was brought to California by Chinese immigrants. Due to its preference for disturbed soil, it follows the hand of man closely, often growing in new developments, new roadways and industrial areas. It gained a foothold in Europe after WWI and WWII, when it grew out of bomb craters and the rubble of destroyed cities. It currently flourishes in many war-torn areas of the world.

Although it was first prized by gardeners, it soon became a pest, propagating quickly and taking over entire forests. It forces out native species by producing a chemical that discourages growth by other plants. Besides its worldwide distribution, it is firmly established in the U.S. and is now classified as an invasive species in thirty states, including California. It is very hard to kill. Simply cutting it off at the base actually encourages runners to spread and sprout. Herbicide treatments can be effective, but need constant rechecking of treated areas, as the tree has a remarkable ability to re-grow from its buried roots and runners.

Here in La Crescenta it is common to see it growing next to the flood control channels and debris basins. If you would like to see examples of Ailanthus, there are a couple right on Foothill. A really pretty stand of mature trees is growing behind the small house/business in the lot to the west of Everest Burgers. On the corner of Foothill and Sunset is a great example of how quickly the tree can dominate an area. A developer tore a house down a few years ago, and Ailanthus started growing immediately in the vacant lot. The property owner had them cut down but they grew right back. If you peek over the construction fence there, you will see probably over a hundred trees growing there. Ailanthus has taken root in the author's yard, his mom's yard, his daughter's, and his father-in-law's yard. Chances are Ailanthus will come to live with you as well.

Our Glorious Yuccas

In springtime, our hillsides are accented with the spectacular flowering of tall yucca plants. They stand out from our native chaparral, literally, as they rapidly shoot up above the low, dark-green canopy to a height of 6 or 10 feet and explode with thick creamy-white flowers. Just glance at our hillsides in the spring to spot them, vertical splashes of white.

The yucca goes by a lot of names, all with interesting origins, and all related to the settlement of California. The word "yucca" was mistakenly applied to our plants by the Spanish explorers. Our yuccas share a resemblance with the cassava plant in the Caribbean, called "yuca" by the native people there. Early American settlers of California called it the "Lord's candle" (because of its flame-shape when flowering) or "Spanish bayonet" (because of its sharp leaf-points), both a romantic reference to the California Mission era. Even its Latin name, *Hesperoyucca whipplei*, has American settlement roots. It is named for Amiel Whipple, a surveyor for the Pacific Railroad coming to California in the 1850s.

Our local native yuccas are related to a wide variety of plants, with vastly different shapes. For example, Joshua trees are a form of yucca, as are several small yard landscaping plants that are currently quite popular in drought-tolerant yard plantings.

One fun fact about the yucca is the symbiotic relationship it has with a particular insect, the aptly-named yucca moth. Each spring, when the yucca flowers blossom, the male and female yucca moths meet for a romantic rendezvous at the local yucca, which acts as a natural singles bar. When the female is ready to lay eggs, she collects pollen from a yucca flower, then flies to another yucca. She lays her eggs in the new flower, then packs the collected pollen on top of the eggs, thus pollinating the flower, so that it will produce seeds. Once the seeds start growing, the moth eggs hatch; the baby moths eat a few seeds, leaving several others intact for future propagation. They then burrow out and drop to the ground, where they cocoon up to hatch the next spring. The yucca is exclusively pollinated by the yucca moth, and the yucca moth only eats yucca seeds. They cannot survive without each other.

The Native Americans made extensive use of the yucca. Probably its main use was for cordage. The long leaves of the yucca are extremely fibrous. The leaves were soaked in water or warmed over fire, then pounded gently with a rock until the stringy fibers broke apart into individual strands. The strands were braided, and any number of items could be produced with the resulting string. String, ropes, nets, blankets, clothing, sandals, and baskets were all produced with the fiber of yucca leaves. As well, the leaves have a coating that was used as a soap by the native people. The rest of the yucca was used as a food source. The bulb at the base of the plant was roasted and eaten like a potato. The stalks were prepared and eaten in the same way. The flowers were eaten after rinsing to remove the bitterness, but the fruit was eaten raw. The seeds were roasted and pounded into flour. It was a well-used plant. Even the thorn at the end of the leaves was used as a tool for sewing or making holes.

Medicinal uses of yucca were many for the Native Americans, the plant bordering on a "cure all". Digestion, arthritis, headaches, asthma, high blood pressure – you name it, and yucca treated it. Its use continues today in some supplements and is found in some veterinary medicines.

Yet for us here in the valley, the yuccas of our surrounding mountains are simply pleasing to the eye. Once you know their history, they are a wonderful link to our past as well.

Our Mountains Once Had Thick Pine Forests

The south face of the San Gabriel Mountains that loom over our valley are stark and majestic. In the late afternoon when the slanting sunlight brings out the pinks and oranges of the rock faces, our mountains look very much like desert mountains, bare and rocky like those above Palm Springs or Death Valley.

Yet that was not always the case. The mountain faces above us used to be interspersed with deep green, and boasted thick forests of a conifer unique to Southern California, the bigcone Douglas fir. Dense stands of 50–100-foot-tall trees blanketed each canyon.

Cook, Dunsmore, Shields, and most spectacularly Pickens Canyon were cool and shaded under the cover of thousands of trees. They would have been thick near the stream beds, diminishing into patches and single trees up the steep canyon walls nearly to the ridgelines and peaks. How far down they crept into the valley floor we do not know, but since the lower elevation for these trees is 1,000 feet, we can guess that at least a few of them grew in the streambeds that snaked across the alluvial fans that make up our valley floor.

Bigcone Douglas firs are quite unique. This larger relative to the common Douglas fir is extremely limited in its range, occurring exclusively in the mountain ranges near the coast of Southern California, and nowhere else in the world. Their range extends only from San Diego County north as far as Santa Barbara, and as far inland as Tehachapi and Kern County. They're well suited to our climate, being drought-tolerant and wild-fire resistant. The trees have good longevity and within stands of surviving bigcones, 250-years-old and older is commonplace. One tree sampled yielded an age of 622 years, and larger and presumably older trees exist that have not had their ages measured. The largest known bigcone, dubbed "Old Glory" grows in San Antonio Canyon near Mt. Baldy, and was measured (before a storm took the top off) at 145 feet tall.

Although now missing from our mountains (a few lone giants can still be spotted high in our canyons), they can easily be viewed on the backside of our range. Take a drive up Big Tujunga Canyon or Angeles Crest Highway and look into the north and east facing canyons along the highway. Those tall dark pines you see clumped in the ravines are likely the bigcones, and looking at these forested canyons you can envision what the mountains over our valley must have looked like.

The bigcone Douglas fir has a very distinctive look to it, and once one learns its characteristics, they are instantly recognizable. They have a ragged, sparse appearance, and their branches tend to droop downward, rather than turning upward like other pines. This drooping look led to its miscatagorization as a spruce tree by pioneers, and one often reads in early stories of the "bigcone spruce" that was here for only a short time after the white man first arrived.

What happened to all the trees? Quite simply and as you may already guess—logging—but why did they not grow back? Too many fires? Erosion? Smog? Whatever the reason, there is hope for the future. We have a group of visionaries here in our valley who want to restore at least one of our canyons back the dense cool forest it once was. This group of volunteers, organized under the leadership of Glendale Park Department's Trails and Open Space program, has in the last few years planted and watered many bigcone fir saplings in Deukmejian Park, and more plantings are planned. The city staff and volunteers have tracked down nurseries that are growing baby bigcones and are caring for the seedlings at the park. When you go to the park, envision the park's trails in twenty years, cool and shady from the big trees. It will be just like looking into the past.

Mud Flow, Debris Flow ... What's the Difference?

It is important to understand the ground we have built our homes on here in the Crescenta Valley. We live on layer after layer of alluvial fan. The San Gabriel Mountains are some of the fastest growing, and the fastest decomposing mountains in the world. They are made of brittle, decomposing granite, which fractures with each earthquake like safety glass. All those chunks of granite fall down into the canyons, along with the sand from the decomposing rocks. When it rains hard, those chunks of rock and sand are carried out across the valley, fanning out from the canyon mouths, thus the term "alluvial fan." Those chunks of rock are what we encounter when we attempt to dig holes in our yards.

In a rainstorm, the faster the water comes down the mountain, the more rocks it can carry. Newly denuded mountains from wildfires ensure that the water, with no foliage and roots to slow its downhill flow, will be moving very fast by the time it reaches the rock-filled canyons.

A little water in the canyons carries mud, the water being strong enough to push only fine grains of sand—mud flow. Larger amounts of water can move small stones, then larger rocks, then boulders as it grows in volume—debris flow.

This is the fundamental difference between the dynamic of a "mud flow" and "debris flow." As the amount of particulates increase in the flow of water, and the speed increases, there comes a weird tipping point where the physics of the flow changes completely. The larger rocks begin to "float" on the churning material below it, allowing them to pick up speed, and in some cases surf the front of the flow. This creates a churning wall of mud and boulders that can move quite fast—30, 40, or 50 miles per hour. It is that churning mass that tore some bodies into pieces back in our big New Year's Flood in 1934.

This mass, which geologists call a "slug," cannot be stopped by anything man-made. That is why in photos of the 1934 flood you see bare foundations from which houses were sheared off, as though by a gigantic bulldozer. The debris flow turns back into a mud flow only when it slows down enough for the rocks to drop out, while the mud and water continue on.

The main purpose of debris basins that sit at the mouth of all our canyons is to serve as a speed bump for debris slugs. Once the slug hits the basin, it pauses long enough for the rocks to drop out, and the water and mud can continue down the flood control channel. If the basin is full, the slug does not stop, and it overwhelms the channel below, fanning out across the valley like it has for hundreds of thousands of years.

The phenomenon of debris flow is very unpredictable. It has happened on a huge scale in pre-history (again, that is where the rocks in your yard came from), and we know it will happen again.

We have built our homes in harm's way. We cannot predict major debris flows, but we can say when they are more likely. L.A. County and Glendale have been very clear with residents here. Debris flows cannot be predicted and cannot be fully controlled. We just have to get out of the way.